Before&After
GRAPHICS
FOR BUSINESS

by JOHN McWADE

Peachpit Press

Before & After Graphics for Business
John McWade

Peachpit Press
1249 Eighth Street
Berkeley, CA 94710
510/524-2178
510/524-2221 (fax)

Find us on the World Wide Web at: **www.peachpit.com**
To report errors, please send a note to errata@peachpit.com

Peachpit Press is a division of Pearson Education

Editor: Cathy Fishel
Production editor: Lupe Edgar
Compositor: Kim Scott
Indexer: Joy Dean Lee
Cover design: John McWade
Interior design: Kim Scott

ISBN 0-321-33415-9

9 8 7 6 5 4

Printed and bound in the United States of America

Acknowledgements

Thank you for your wonderful response to my first book, *Before & After Page Design.* Your readership is what inspired this second book. Because both are derived from our magazine *Before & After, How to design cool stuff* and both are produced by the same staff, I will begin by making with gratitude the same acknowledgements.

I will thank first our friend and business partner Michael Solomon, without whom we wouldn't be here. And so many thank-you's must go to the countless *Before & After* subscribers who have written to us over the years. We read and still save every letter, and although we respond to very few personally (it would simply be a full-time job!), I must say that your encouragement and support have been incredibly strengthening.

Thank you very much to *Before & After* magazine staff and contributors both present and past whose work you'll see on these pages. In alphabetical order let me acknowledge Chuck Donald, Rebecca George, Laura Lamar, and John Odam, and set aside for special mention Gwen Amos, (whose influence has been immeasurable) and Chuck Green. I'm also happy to acknowledge the good work of our young, new designers Vincent Pascual and Dexter Mark Abellera, who are the first of those who will be taking *Before & After* into the next generation.

As before, I am delighted to thank the hardworking crew at Peachpit Press—Cathy Fishel, our editor; Kim Scott, our designer; Marjorie Baer, our liaison; Nancy Ruenzel, publisher; Lupe Edgar, production editor; and Suzie Lowey for helping track myriad files coming and going.

And once again, thank you to the most important person in my life, my wife Gaye, who's worked and walked with me step by step through dangers, toils, and snares for more than 30 years. Gaye is the most *original thinker* I know. With her I can see the deep things in life, the things that matter, where God is. In places where I would embrace ordinary cultural fizz and imagine it cool, she shows me the new and the real. She nurtures, challenges, and keeps me focused, and without her there never would have been a *Before & After* magazine.

Table of contents

Foreword

Graphic design has many definitions. It is sometimes used to mean *decoration,* as in decorating a birthday cake or a room. A decoration is an add-on, an embellishment made to delight the eye. Decoration is not essential. The cake will taste the same with or without its decoration.

To some, graphic design is a means of *self-expression.* "I am an arteest; I make design." Design of this sort is usually done for personal enrichment, like painting. You see on Web logs—or blogs—a lot of self-expressive graphic design. You also see it on T-shirts and even in spray paint on the sides of railroad cars.

Design on a computer is often used to mean *production,* that is, the point-and-click of making graphics software do something. To say, "I designed a Web page," often means, "I placed the images, typed the copy, connected the links and coded the HTML." But that's not design; it's construction. It is to design what wiring the house is to architecture.

The title of this book is *Graphics for Business.* By graphics for business, we mean design as *business communication.* You design graphics for business when you have a message to make, an idea to get across, even a pose to strike.

At *Before & After,* we say that good design meets three criteria: beauty, simplicity, and clarity.

In business, certainly, your graphics must be beautiful. Often, a viewer's response to your business is formed in a few moments by what he or she first sees.

If your message is complex, you use design to simplify it.

If an idea is difficult to understand, you use design to clarify it.

The best design is all three: beautiful, simple, clear.

At Before & After, *we say that good design meets three criteria: beauty, simplicity, and clarity.*

Graphics for business are the kind that most of us make every day. Charts, newsletters, stationery, forms, calendars, and other ordinary documents comprise the bulk of all business communication.

Graphics for business are graphics with their feet in the real world.

Introduction

The hard work it takes to make good design is almost universally underestimated. Even to designers, design looks easier than it is. To many people, design looks easy enough for a child to do. Reality, however, is very different. In the same way, we are often unaware of the value of design. Design has real power. The irony is how oblivious we can be to the influence of design while making many of our own buying decisions based solely on how things look.

As design gets closer to home, however, reality begins to dawn. This can be illustrated by a funny story that we first published in *Before & After* magazine.

Reader Darrell Jamieson of Broken Arrow, Oklahoma, sent us the following clip from an issue of the *Tulsa World* newspaper:

"Just when it looked like Tulsa County's mayors and commissioners were working smoothly on the new Tulsa jail trust authority, an impasse has developed.

"The Tulsa County Criminal Justice Authority members can't agree on what the group's letterhead should look like.

"County Commissioner Bob Dick, chairman of the seven-member jail authority, wanted the group to have its own letterhead, so officials would not have to use county letterheads when mailing materials to other government agencies or companies involved in building the jail.

"At a Jan. 12 meeting, Dick submitted three designs to other members of the authority, thinking one would be accepted with little discussion. However, four members, including Tulsa Mayor Susan Savage, rejected the designs.

"One of the designs, a triangular logo with the authority's name over the motto 'Dedicated to Community Safety,' looked 'too much like a road sign,' in the words of County Commissioner Lewis Harris.

"Another design, which featured the authority's acronym superimposed over a set of jail bars, was 'too artsy,' Harris said.

"Owasso Mayor Charles Burris also noted that every city in the county except his was

Even to designers, design looks easier than it is.

included in the three designs.

"Dick concluded, 'We want a non-artsy-craftsy, dynamic logo that doesn't look like a road sign.'

"Although jail authority members joke about disagreement over the letterhead, they admit that picking a symbol to represent the group is taking a little longer than they had thought it would.

"With a few exceptions, members have agreed on several key points in the jail-building process so far, including unanimously picking a law firm to represent the authority.

"On Friday, members saw two new designs, one from Burris with Hollywood Western lettering and another from county staffers with the motto 'TCCJA: Justice for Green Country's Second Century.'

"'I don't really care what it looks like, but I'm not sure that [motto] is something I'd like to go along with,' County Commissioner John Selph said after the meeting.

"Savage also wants to submit designs.

"'We're not graphic artists, but it's clear we want to have something simple but functional,' she said. 'This is just a housekeeping thing we need to get done.'"

NBC television once paid a designer a million dollars to design an N.

There you have it. A fellow submits three designs to his colleagues who embrace his idea but reject his art. One town mayor responds with his own design, and another wants to submit hers. Never mind this was about a letterhead. What's funny is that all of it is perfectly normal.

Design is more significant than it looks. It's definitely not "housekeeping." Why would the mayor offer to do the housekeeping? How can this group agree on legal counsel but not on the housekeeping? Why do all have an opinion about the housekeeping?

"I don't really care what it looks like," said one commissioner. What he doesn't see is that he actually does.

We all do. Design is personal. How we look tells the world who and what we are.

The commissioner doesn't care what his letterhead looks like in the way that a designer would. But the right look will speak to him, and the looks he saw didn't.

This is what I mean when I say design has a voice.

This voice can be heard everywhere. It drives the vast apparel, accessories, and cosmetics industry (we're designing our selves). It drives the auto industry. It drives the building industry. It drives the consumer-products industries.

Before he was back at Apple, when Steve Jobs started his Next computer company, his *first act*—before he had a building, before he had employees, before he had a product—was to pay Paul Rand $100,000 to design a logo. And Rand's black cube gave Next its sleek identity.

NBC television once paid a designer a million dollars to design an N.

Tulsa's mayor calls for a letterhead that is "simple but functional." What she means (or hopes) is a color or shape or a few lines that embody and express, for all to see, the jail trust's abiding attributes: dignity, service, competence, integrity.

To find this, though, we must look up toward the light, not down toward the dust mop.

Graphics for business take time, they take effort, they take study, and they even take a book.

Everything rides on the outcome.

Happy designing.

Newsletters

Is your newsletter displayed in a public place? Here are six simple ways to improve its *curb appeal*.

Catch the eye of a passerby

Sierra Adoption Services is a private agency with a big job on its hands. Adopting a child is a major step for anyone, but SAS specializes in placing children who are least likely to be chosen naturally—older kids, members of sibling groups who need to stay together, developmentally delayed or otherwise challenged children, and so on.

It's crucial to get the stories of these children out to adults who might possibly welcome them home. That's where SAS' *Homecoming* newsletter comes in. *Homecoming* dispenses news to donors and adoptive families, but it also serves as a key recruiting tool. Its target is the adult new to the idea of adoption. Its creator strives to make the newsletter appealing enough that a casual passerby at a county fair booth or other public function might pick it up and be drawn in.

A newsletter that attracts from a distance? It's a familiar sight to any convention-goer, but how is it done? By taking a tip from newsstand magazines and working in big bold strokes.

BEFORE

An issue full of attractive photos—but none is on the cover!
No image in commercial design has more appeal than the human face—and none more than that of a child. Yet here is a newsletter whose most attractive features are hidden inside. First step: Move these photos to the front page.

A grid of eight columns yields flexibility

Most newsletters are full of visual detail—text, dates, a table of contents, captions, headlines, subheads, callouts, boxes, borders, rules, bangs, and, often, photographs. The only way to keep order in such a busy house is to set up a flexible structure—in this case, an eight-column grid. Every object aligns to a grid column; the narrowest object will be one column wide, while the widest can be as many as eight. Most fall in between.

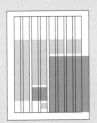 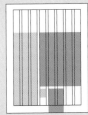 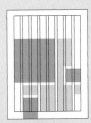

Equal columns. Text in four equal columns is the most uniform. Such narrow columns should be set in a condensed typeface, or in very small point sizes.

Unequal columns. Here, text spans three columns and a photo spans five; any combination can work. Note how the tiny photo and caption cling to the grid.

Empty outer margins. Here the grid's versatility begins to reveal itself; two outer columns remain empty to catch overflow from the inner six. It's asymmetrical.

Four steps to an expressive nameplate

Our nameplate's bouncy, kid-like quality is an easy style to mimic. It lends itself best to bold, block typefaces with little detail. Getting the fore-aft effect of its various letters is easiest in a draw program in which the letters can be converted from fonts to graphic objects.

1. Rough it in
Set your type in approximately its final size (note here the first letter is about 20% larger) and kern until the letters overlap; the exact amount isn't important yet.

2. Tint
Convert to paths, then tint letters in alternating shades of gray. Four shades are usually enough; we've used 75%, 60%, 45%, and 30%.

3. Bounce
Push letters up and down, and adjust side to side until the final fit is just so. This step requires some artful randomness, but very little actual movement.

4. Shadow
A black shadow heightens contrast. Duplicate the entire line of text, color the duplicate black, and send it to the back. Offset a point or two, usually to the right and down.

Make eye contact

Nothing stops our eyes as fast as another set of eyes making direct contact; it is the most arresting of all visual images. If you have such a photo, use it. Below right is the easiest way: Scale it up big enough to seem life-size—here it covers seven of our eight columns—then add text. Text in a box is a versatile way to manage type and photo in the same space. (**1**) Fit box to grid, then indent text one pica or so; (**2**) a round dot is a visual counterpoint to the rectangles. It falls off the grid deliberately, giving the impression of a casual stamp.

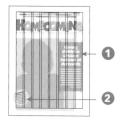

1999 Objective Graphs 3 **Adoption Clinic 3** AAP Alert 7 **Coming Events 7** Family Network Program 3 **Gift Drive Results 5** Recent Placements 6 **Thank You's 4** Valentines Offer 8 **Wish List 5**

HOMECOMING

SIERRA ADOPTION SERVICES NEWSLETTER

Giving children choices instead of demands

Parents who want to gain control must first give away a little control. This means giving their children choices instead of demands whenever possible.

One of the most often asked questions about choic-

continued on page 2

SIERRA ADOPTION SERVICES provides permanent adoptive families for children with special needs. Turn to page 6 to meet Michael and his new family.

SPECIAL THANKS TO LECTRAMEDIA WHO DONATED THE PRINTING OF THIS NEWSLETTER.

Without eye contact, she's cuddly, but less engaging; be sure to have such images looking *into* the page. Narrow photo accommodates more text; rectangular box in lower right is an important visual counterweight.

Draw a mask

A photographic mask removes the background and brings the subject front and center. This is a very effective way to arrest the attention of a viewer. Around people, the mask leaves a curvy, organic shape that contrasts beautifully with the sharp, rectangular edges of the page. Note, below left, that type shares space by overprinting the masked photo.

The ideal photo can be masked completely. But if your photo is partially cropped, mask the remainder, then abut the cropped sides to the edges of the page or to an artificial line like a column rule you create.

Gang up

Here, three photos take the place of one. What's important about this is that the photos are tightly clustered and so work as a single focal point—you want them connected either by proximity or by line of sight. In this case, the vertical gray bar and the angled dot reinforce the group.

In any such group, all heads should be the same size and cropped the same way. If one is different, it will clearly look out of place.

Be sure all head shots are sized and cropped the same.

Groups
For curb appeal, the more clustered your photos, the more effective they will be. Note here that regardless of size and arrangement, the photos remain adjoined.

Mix and match

This treatment balances a masked image with the visual weight of a tight cluster. Text fluidly fills the space between, making a unified whole. This is an excellent way to deal with several related photos; by elevating one to a focal point, they reinforce rather than compete. It's also practical: You must mask only a single image to turn an ordinary layout into something special. Select an image with a relatively simple edge.

Above, a sophisticated variation connects the masked photo directly to the group and adds a tiny masked photo for visual intrigue. The gray caption serves as a pivot; note that both masked images touch it.

Set an artful headline…

What design resource is always available and endlessly mutable? Type, of course! This supersize headline has the eye-stopping pull of a traffic sign and the added allure of being *unexpected.* Set it first in your headline typeface, then try a text face, which at this size will often reveal surprising style. In either case, the rule is to space letters much tighter than normal. But no rule says every word must be the same size: They can vary according to style, fit, and what they say. Another attribute: A headline this big can be placed anywhere. We have it in the upper left, but the lower right, for example, would work just as well.

Aligned right   Centered

Giving Children
Choices
Instead of
Demands

Giving Children
Choices
Instead
—of—
Demands

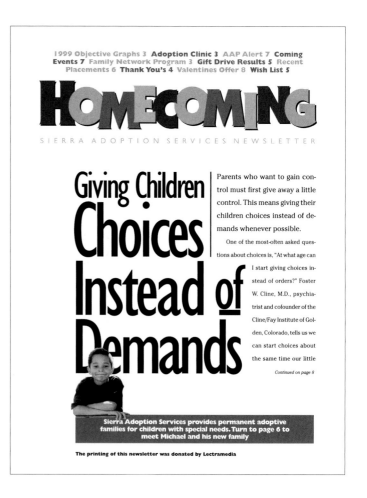

HOMECOMING

SIERRA ADOPTION SERVICES NEWSLETTER

Giving Children
Choices
Instead of
Demands

Parents who want to gain control must first give away a little control. This means giving their children choices instead of demands whenever possible.

One of the most-often asked questions about choices is, "At what age can I start giving choices instead of orders?" Foster W. Cline, M.D., psychiatrist and cofounder of the Cline/Fay Institute of Golden, Colorado, tells us we can start choices about the same time our little

Continued on page 8

Sierra Adoption Services provides permanent adoptive families for children with special needs. Turn to page 6 to meet Michael and his new family

The printing of this newsletter was donated by Lectramedia

...or a giant initial cap!

This solution is the easiest of all, yet one of the most engaging. Its dominant graphic element is a REALLY BIG initial letter. Here it's been tinted gray to not overpower the page, although note that a photo has been carefully positioned to keep the layout in balance.

A letter this big can be very decorative; it's a good place to try styles with elaborate swashes and fine detail that would otherwise be lost. The most common style, though, matches either the nameplate (shown here), or the headline or text typestyles.

Balance A heavy visual element high on the page will upset the equilibrium unless it's offset by a similar weight, in this case, the photo on the bottom. Here, the result is an engaging contrast of simple and complex—the plain letter catches the eye, while photo and text beneath it form a detailed point of interest.

How to pick, set, and lay out type that can be *read*.

What typefaces are best for text?

Text type is more common than any other. Text makes up the acres of gray in books, magazines, reports, and hundreds of other documents. When *reading* is the primary goal, it's the designer's job to ensure the text is as smooth and pleasant as possible. The hallmarks of good text type are *legibility* and *readability*.

Legibility refers to clarity; it's how readily one letter can be distinguished from all others. Readability refers to how well letters interact to compose words, sentences, and paragraphs. When evaluating the choices, your operative word is *medium*.

1   Pick fonts with similar character widths

To flow most smoothly, an alphabet's characters should have similar widths. Reading has a natural rhythm; an alphabet such as Futura (right) with widely varying character widths, disrupts it.

FUTURA LIGHT

TIMES NEW ROMAN

2   Medium height-to-width ratio

We identify letters by their physical characteristics—stems, bars, loops, curves, and so on; the clearer they are the more legible the letter. As letters are compressed (or expanded), these features get distorted—diagonal strokes, for example, become quite vertical—and are harder to identify.

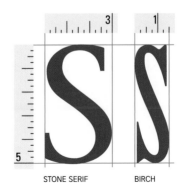

STONE SERIF   BIRCH

The x-height of a typestyle is the height of its lowercase characters. The larger the x-height, the denser the type will appear. You want *medium*; unusually tall or short x-heights are better suited for specialty projects.

COCHIN   TIMES NEW ROMAN

x-height variations

Adobe Caslon   Century Expanded   Helvetica Neue   Cochin

Serif or sans serif: Which is easier to read?

Conventional wisdom holds that for large amounts of text—a solid page or more—serif type is easier than sans serif for the reader to deal with. There are a few theories why. First is simply that it's what we're most accustomed to; the text of virtually all newspapers, magazines, and books is set in serif type. The idea holds water: In countries where sans serif type predominates (like Sweden), sans serif type is what readers say they prefer.

Second is that serif type is more organic; its strokes are graceful combinations of thicks and thins very similar to natural penmanship (below left). Sans serif typestyles, in contrast, are prized for their cold, high-tech, machine-like qualities. Their geometric shapes literally require mechanical instruments to draw (below center).

Third is that serifs create physical bridges between letters that quietly lead the eye from one letter to the next (below right).

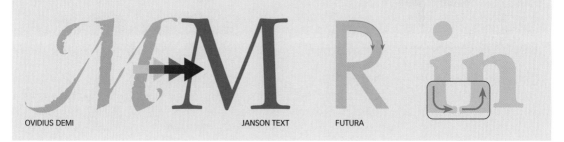

OVIDIUS DEMI   JANSON TEXT   FUTURA

4   Avoid overlarge counters

Counters are the enclosed spaces inside letters. Avoid typestyles whose counters are very large in relation to the stroke weight. In the case of Avant Garde, note how much greater the space inside the letters is than the space outside. This will slow the reader; set in text, Avant Garde would look like Swiss cheese!

Lorem ipsum dolor sit amet, conse adipscing elit, diam nonnumy eiu tempor incidunt ut labore et dolo gna aliquam erat volupat. Ut enir minimim veniami quis nostrud exer ullamcorper suscipit laboris nisl ut ex ea commodo consequat. Duis vel eum irure dolor in reprehende voluptate velit esse molestaie son

AVANT GARDE

5   Watch out for mirrors

Geometric typestyles are so uniform, their letters are often mirror images (right). For text, this is not ideal—the more distinct each letter is, the more legible whole words will be. Look for typestyles that don't mirror, such as Gill Sans (below).

GILL SANS

HELVETICA NEUE 55

Favorite text faces

While many typefaces meet the requirements of legibility, readability, and beauty, the following eight are ones that work extremely well.

Lorem ipsum dolor sit amet, consectetur admod tempor incidunt u labore et dolore r enim ad minimim veniami quis nostrud exercition ullamcorper suscipit laboris nisl ut aliquip ex ea commodo consequat. Duis autem vel eum irure dolor in reprehenderit in voluptate velit esse molestaie son consequat, vel illum dolore eu fugiat

9-PT ON 10.5 PT LEADING

Adobe Caslon

First choice for books, Caslon is probably the Roman alphabet's most readable typeface. Its letters aren't beautiful, but strung into sentences and paragraphs, they have fit, texture, bite, and can be read comfortably for hours. Caslon will withstand even the tightest leading.

Lorem ipsum dolor sit amet, consectetur admod tempor incidunt u labore et dolore r enim ad minimim veniami quis nostrud exercition ullamcorper suscipit laboris nisl ut aliquip ex ea commodo consequat. Duis autem vel eum irure dolor in reprehenderit in voluptate velit esse molestaie son consequat, vel illum dolore eu fugiat

9.3-PT ON 10.5-PT LEADING

Adobe Garamond

If they could pick only one face, for many designers, this would be it: Garamond is easy to read and elegant, too. It's a fine display face—rare in this class—and as a result can carry a document all by itself. Garamond sets small; set in 10-point minimum with about 10-percent extra leading.

Lorem ipsum dolor sit amet, consectetur a ing elit, diam no mod tempor incidunt dunt ut labore et lupat. Ut enim ad minimim veniami quis nostrud exercitation ullamcorper suscipit laboris nisl ut aliquip ex ea commodo consequat. Duis autem vel eum irure dolor in reprehenderit in voluptate velit esse molestaie son consequat, vel illum do-

7.8-PT ON 10.5-PT LEADING

Stone Serif

Stone can be boring to look at but buttery to read. Characterized by its stubby, lowercase *r* that tucks snugly to its neighbors, Stone is designed for outstanding *fit*. It sets large; 9-point is as big as you should go. Use at least 35-percent extra leading.

Lorem ipsum dolor sit amet, consectetur ad ing elit, diam nor mod tempor incidunt ut labore et dolo Ut enim ad minimim veniami quis nostrud exercitation ullamcorper suscipit laboris nisl ut aliquip ex ea commodo consequat. Duis autem vel eum irure dolor in reprehenderit in voluptate velit esse molestaie son consequat, vel illum dolore

8.8-PT ON 10.5-PT LEADING

Janson Text

Janson holds the middle ground between the earthy, workmanlike nature of Caslon and the high classiness of Garamond. Rounder and denser, it has a chiseled, resolute appearance. Janson sets about average size; give it about 20-percent extra leading.

Lorem ipsum dolor sit elit, diam nonnumy e labore et dolore mag

Lorem ipsum dolor si elit, diam nonnumy e labore et dolore mag

Lorem ipsum dolor sit elit, diam nonnumy e labore et dolore mag

Lorem ipsum dolor sit elit, diam nonnumy e labore et dolore mag

Times New Roman

A navy blazer; *always* acceptable.

Bembo

Sharp-edged classic. Too stylish for all jobs.

Glypha

Outstanding slab-serif. Best fit in typedom.

Frutiger

Glypha's sans-serif cousin. Fast reading.

6   Look for small variations in stroke weight

The best text faces have stroke weights that vary somewhat. These help distinguish each letter from its neighbors. Avoid extremes. *Modern* styles (such as Bodoni) vary too much; at high resolution their beautiful, superthin strokes disappear in a dazzle. Sleek *geometric* styles (such as Futura) vary little or not at all, so are too uniform.

BAUER BODONI   TIMES NEW ROMAN   FUTURA

Lorem ipsum dolor sit amet, consectet scing elit, diam nonnumy eiusmod ter incidunt ut labore et dolore magna ali erat volupat. Ut enim ad minimim veni nostrud exercitation ullamcorper suscipi nisl ut aliquip ex ea commodo consequ autem vel eum irure dolor in repreher voluptate velit esse molestaie son cons vel illum dolore eu fugiat nulla pariat

BAUER BODONI

Lorem ipsum dolor sit amet, consectetur a elit, diam nonnumy eiusmod tempor inci labore et dolore magna aliquam erat volu enim ad minimim veniami quis nostrud exe ullamcorper suscipit laboris nisl ut aliqu commodo consequat. Duis autem vel eur dolor in reprehenderit in voluptate velit lestaie son consequat, vel illum dolore e nulla pariatur. Ut enim ad minimim venia

TIMES NEW ROMAN

7   Avoid quirkiness

Typographic sprites are fun to look at and great for heads, but in text they wear out their welcome fast. Why? The extra swashiness gives the eye too much to follow. Very tiring.

BELWE

Letters, words, and whole lines must be spaced to flow in a smooth, natural way. There are three kinds of spacing: the spaces between letters, or *letter spacing*; the space between words, or *word spacing*; and the space between lines, called *leading* (pronounced *ledding*). In most cases, page layout software defaults will produce nearly ideal text spacing with no input from you.

Medium word spacing is best

When type is well set, we read words not individually but in clumps: Word spacing controls the speed with which we can get hold of the clumps. Most readers are most comfortable when the distance between words is about the space normally occupied by a lowercase *i*. Less than that and words run together (**1**); more and they drift apart (**2**). Most page-layout software defaults to this amount; word processing software tends to set words too loose.

ADOBE GARAMOND

❶
Word spacing should b
enough to allow for lett
group into individual w
With too little space, w
the text run together. Te
too much space makes
choppy reading becaus

❷
Word spacing shoul
large enough to all
for letters to group
individual words. W
too little space, wor
the text run togethe
Text with too much

Medium letter spacing is best

Every letter has a subliminal rhythm created by its alternating positive and negative spaces (the *ink* and *non-ink* area). As a rule for text, the space between the strokes of two letters should not be less than the width of a letter's stroke, or this natural rhythm will be lost (**1**). Similarly, if the space is too great (**2**), the letters will visually disconnect. As with word spacing, page-layout software usually defaults to good text letterspacing; word-processing software most often sets letters too loose.

ITC GARAMOND

❶
Lorem ipsum dolor sit am
consectetur adipscing elit,
nonnumy eiusmod tempo

❷
Lorem ipsum dol
amet, consectetu
adipscing elit, dia

Start with 120% leading

A good rule of thumb for text is to set leading 120% of the type size. Set 10-point type, for example, on 12-point leading. A typeface with a tall x-height should be looser, a short x-height tighter. If your leading is the same as your type size, it's said to be *solid* (which is quite tight). Tight lines generally appear urgent and newsy, loose lines airy and elegant.

ADOBE CASLON

Lorem ipsum dolor sit amet adipscing elit, diam nonnumy por incidunt ut labore et dol aliquam erat volupat. Ut enim veniami quis nostrud exercita per suscipit laboris nisl ut aliq

ADOBE CASLON 10/11

Lorem ipsum dolor sit amet adipscing elit, diam nonnumy por incidunt ut labore et dol aliquam erat volupat. Ut enim veniami quis nostrud exercita

ADOBE CASLON 10/15

Set text in caps and lowercase

Text set in lowercase is easier and more pleasant to read than in all caps. That's because lowercase letters have more variety, and their ascenders and descenders create unique word shapes which the eye can identify quickly.

TEXT SET IN ALL CAPS IS CUMBERSOME BECAUSE THE SHAPE OF INDIVIDUAL WORDS ALL LOOK THE SAME. WORDS MUST THEN BE READ LETTER BY LETTER, SLOWING THE READING PROCESS CONSIDERABLY.

CENTURY OLD STYLE

This strong structure shows off well, and it's perfect for in-office printing.

Design a handsome, 'no frills' newsletter

Busy readers must make value judgments at a glance. The newsletter we feature here goes to about 150 people who use the services of a university's computer department. It is a captive audience, but that fact does not change the designer's job: to make the news inviting, convincing, and easy to read.

What it does affect is the way the newsletter is produced. *Infocraft* is output on a 600-dpi laser printer and is photocopied onto 11 × 17-inch paper and folded.

What kind of design wins the reader's immediate respect, goes together easily, conveys the news quickly, and copies cleanly? Let's see.

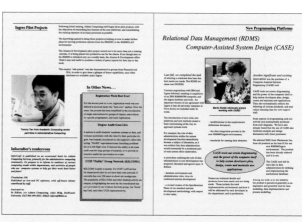

BEFORE: Trying a casual look
This newsletter's designer knew that the subject matter of the publication can be a bit imposing. So for *Infocraft*, he wanted the professional look of a rigid front page, but a friendlier look inside. What happened? The first page is orderly enough, but inside the mixed column widths and headline styles, plus miles of unorganized white space, just created a look of disarray: Each page looks like it comes from a different newsletter.

An effective design should have a repetitive format: Columns, margins, and typestyles form a structure just like a physical building. The way to be more casual is with pictures, callouts, and other visual devices.

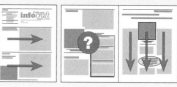

Different formats result in disarray and misdirection.

Dalhousie infocraft

A News Bulletin from UCIS Admin Computing
Issue 1
November 2003

Re-inventing the major administrative systems. . .

The *Administrative Computing Plan* is now well and truly under way. This five-year plan includes the conversion of all major administrative systems to operate on unix computers (as opposed to the current central mainframe system); the introduction of a relational database management system (Ingres); and an eventual capability to integrate the administration of all university data.

The specialist groups working in this area have undergone a broad training programme, followed by pilot projects whose objectives were to consolidate their understanding of the new environments. Work is now under way on converting smaller systems, namely: *Space Inventory, Telephones,* and *Print Centre.*

There are plans being made for of all the systems now on the IBM4381. Notable among these is the discontinuation of *NetMail,* a long-time favourite of many, now largely replaced in practice by other EMail programs. *ARIS,* another stalwart, will be replaced by *TheSIS (The Student Information System),* a completely revised and re-built system or group of systems.

Implementing the conversion will involve all of Admin Computing staff in some capacity; it should result in the acquisition of state-of-the-art information system skills within our group.

Firsts at Dal?

EMail Discussion List
Radio Data Link

We established our own e-mail list to discuss technical and management issues related to the task of migrating from MVS to unix. Featuring technical ops by Aidan Evans, the list quickly grew to 100 members from other universities in North America and other coun...
UCIS had set up this kin...
taking initiative within a...
ourselves and other univ...

Most of the major bu...
which offers high-speed...
new medium of commun...
Pearson Institute were li...
radio (UHF). Antennas a...
Plant; and between Pear...
frequencies simultaneou...
megabits per second.

Personnel & Payroll...
system". The system, fro...
Personnel department of...
distribution of selected f...

A returning student check...

INFOCRAFT

A NEWS BULLETIN FROM DALHOUSIE UNIVERSITY ADMIN COMPUTING

NOVEMBER ISSUE HIGHLIGHTS: Pilot projects produce instant results for Alumni & Development offices **2** New computing platform speeds programming and offers an exciting array of automated options **3** George MacLennan appointed as Director of Database Operations. Big changes expected **4** More!

REINVENTING THE MAJOR ADMINISTRATIVE SYSTEMS

The Administrative Computing Plan is now well and truly under way. This five-year plan includes the conversion of all major administrative systems to operate on unix computers (as opposed to the current central mainframe system); the introduction of a relational database management system (Ingres); and an eventual capability to integrate the administration of all university data.

The specialist groups working in this area have undergone a broad training programme, followed by pilot projects whose objectives were to consolidate their understanding of the new environments. Work is now under way on converting smaller systems, namely: *Space Inventory, Telephones,* and *Print Centre.*

There are plans being made for conversion of all the systems now on the IBM4381.

Notable among these is the discontinuation of *NetMail,* a long-time favourite of many, now largely replaced in practice by other EMail programs. *ARIS,* another stalwart, will be replaced by *TheSIS* (The Student Information System), a completely revised and rebuilt system or group of systems.

Implementing the conversion will involve all of Admin Computing staff in some capacity or another; it should result in the acquisition of new state-of-the-art information system skills within our group.

FIRSTS AT DAL? EMAIL DISCUSSION LIST, RADIO DATA LINK

We established our own EMail list to discuss technical and management issues related to the task of migrating from MVS to unix. Featuring technical ops by Aidan Evans, the list quickly grew to 100 members from other universities in North America and other countries, and is currently at 150. This was the first time that UCIS had

A returning student checks for available courses.

set up this kind of mailing list, and it gave Dalhousie some exposure as taking initiative within an industry trend, while creating a useful forum for ourselves and other universities.

Most of the major buildings on campus are now linked by optical fibre, which offers high-speed (10 megabits per second) data transmission. This year, a new medium of communication was added to the network: Fenwick Tower and the Pearson Institute were linked to the rest of the campus via ultrahigh-frequency radio (UHF). Antennas are located on the roofs of Fenwick Tower and the Physical Plant; and between Pearson and the

Weldon building. The transmission uses several frequencies simultaneously to provide a high level of stability and reliability at 2 megabits per second.

Personnel & Payroll recently went live with their new "human resources system". The system, from a company called GSI, runs on a Novell network. All Personnel department offices are now linked to this system. Plans call for eventual distribution of selected functions to other departments.

1 Stick to one format

A simple repetitive format is easy to build and pleasing to read. Note, for example, how naturally your eye moves through open space from nameplate to headline. It can do this because page one is in clear, visual groups: nameplate, contents, text. Now in crisp, narrow columns, formerly drab acres of copy suddenly seem bite-sized and inviting. Sans serif type is open and cool.

To do all this, start by setting up a simple grid of columns and hanglines. Hanglines are guides that mark horizontal starting points for type and graphics. This redesign has three: one for the nameplate (**1**), a second for front-page text (**2**), and a third for inside-page text (in this case, top of margin) (**3**).

The magic of the grid is that it helps make design decisions. On each page, type and graphics begin at the same place, column widths are the same, and margins are consistent. This similarity from page to page (right) not only makes your newsletter look well organized, it also adds the aura of credibility and professionalism you want.

Document setup
Page: Letter size, portrait orientation, double-sided, facing pages.
Margins: Inside, 4p0; Outside, 7p0; Top, 12p0; Bottom, 6p0.
Column guides: 4 columns, 1p0 between; Horizontal ruler guides at 4p0, 23p0, and 61p0.

Set up columns and hanglines.

Type in single columns is one smooth flow from beginning to end—ideal for fast, easy reading.

Snap to the grid

Keep your crayons inside the lines!
A grid is effective only if you use it. Snap every element—text, graphics, callouts, rules—to margin and column guides; no creeping beyond or falling short.

Photos should fill columns.
Photographs should fill columns edge to edge; partial-column photos leave unsightly, disruptive gaps.

The original *Infocraft* uses three different headline styles. Problem is, it's at random! Correctly used, a change in typestyle signals a new *kind* of information. The makeover employs one type family for headlines, captions, and text. You want a font (this one is Formata) with three distinct weights (1). Set heads in bold, captions medium, and text light.

All type is on uniform, 12-point leading, too.

Type specs
Headline: 12.5/12 Formata Bold, all caps, align left.
Text/Contents: 9/12 Formata Light, justified, first indent 0p9. **Caption:** 7/12 Formata Medium, align left. **Callout:** 11/18 Formata Bold, align left.

This ultra-simple approach has two big assets. One, it's neat as a pin; turn on Lock to Baseline Grid and each line aligns across the columns (2). Two, it's easy to do; the entire newsletter can be poured in a single text block.

1

Formata

Helvetica Neue

Futura

2

for specific programmes, early registration.

UCIS "PUBLIC" GROUP NETWOR (KILCOM1)

KILCOM1 is quite a succes UCIS' LAN service for dep ments that do not have t

BEFORE

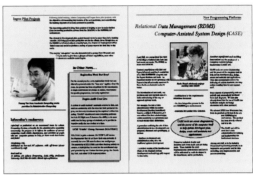

AFTER

High-texture ragged bottoms speed editing and layout

Note text columns end unevenly. This style, called *ragged bottom*, makes your work very easy: No more writing or editing just to fill a column, and no more fine-tuning space at layout time. What's best, though, is it keeps your pages from seeming dense. You can casually break stories into readable, bite-size "packets." The length of each column is up to you. A good rule is to stay within 12 lines of the bottom (1).

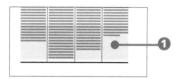

Avoid these ragged-bottom pitfalls:
- Adjacent columns ending at the same place
- Stairsteps that span the page
- Toothless gaps left by a short column trapped between long ones

Design a space-age nameplate

What's a high-tech newsletter without a space-age nameplate? Here's an effective approach: evenly spaced, horizontal lines laid on top of your name.

Set your name in a bold, sans serif font, all caps, and kern it nicely; the tighter it gets, the bolder it will look. Watch for gaps that occur naturally, such as between the *F* and the *O*, and kern more tightly there. Place lines atop the word (here, a 100-pt. name has 1-pt. lines,

4 pts. apart. You may wind up with uneven spaces at the top and bottom (below, middle); the easiest way to even them out is to jimmy the type size. Finally, color the lines to match the background.

Align with natural word breaks if you can. Here, *CRAFT* creates a vertical center axis for the contents; note how the *T* hangs over the right margin.

Readers are drawn to pictures first and read captions before anything else. Make the most of this attention! Write a story for every picture—it will transform the newsletter.

This takes some creative thinking; the idea isn't to write about the picture, necessarily, but to use the pull of the picture to launch your topic. For example, "Sign up for after-hours training" might talk about how training benefited this individual, then about ways in which training could benefit the reader.

No story is as interesting as a human-interest story, and everybody has one. To write it, get involved, be empathetic, and never forget to think, *What does this person mean to our company?*

 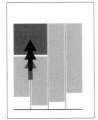   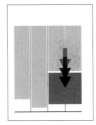

Place photos to go with the flow
Align photos with the top or bottom of the text zone (top is best); their weight will sharpen and help define the design. Always avoid the middle of a column, which blocks the reader's progress.

Callouts are best beneath photos or at tops of columns where text can flow smoothly around them. Mid-column callouts are barriers (far right) to be avoided. Stay away from the bottom, too. On a ragged-bottom page, they look too heavy.

An item-by-item analysis reveals techniques useful for every job.

A newsletter clinic

There are not enough grains of sand in the sea to count the ways in which the elements of a newsletter page can be assembled. There are so many that if you build the page by clicking aimlessly—a headline *here*, a border *there*—your chances for a satisfying result are zero.

What makes a page design good? As in all commercial design, the good page is the one that communicates. Communication means that *the reader receives the message the publisher sends*. This is entirely different from merely being pretty (although pretty is preferable to ugly); it requires more than just clear writing, (although clear writing is vital); and silly as it sounds, it implies that the reader *reads* the page—no reading, no communication. This seems obvious, but most writing is never read simply because of weak or inappropriate design.

Reading asks time, effort, and attention: Your page must appear to be worth the readers' time. If it does not, they will quickly turn elsewhere.

The example we will work with here is an employee newsletter. Note how the redesign transforms the publication from something people might feel obligated to read into something they *want* to read.

Typefaces before
Headlines: Helvetica bold, **Text:** Palatino 10/Auto

Typefaces after
Headlines: Helvetica Inserat (sans serif) or Copperplate 31bc, 32bc, or 33bc (serif),
Text: Adobe Garamond 12/15

TAMS
IN HOUSE
October 2004

S	M	T	W	Th	F	S
	1	2	3	4	5	6
7	8	9	10	11	12	13
14	15	16	17	18	19	20
21	22	23	24	25	26	27
28	29	30	31			

Produced monthly for the employees of TAMS Consultants, Inc.

Harmon Meadow Wetlands Restoration Wins Honor Award in Waterfront Competition

Jury Gives Restoration High Praise

The Harmon Meadow Wetlands Restoration, TAMS' entry in the 2004 Excellence on the Waterfront Award Competition, received an Honor Award at the Waterfront Center's national conference this month. Martin Gold, Hartz Mountain Industries' Director of Planning and Marketing, accepted the award on behalf of TAMS and Hartz Mountain. TAMS Corporate Vice President G. Barrie Heinzenknecht also attended the award presentation and the Waterfront Center conference.

TAMS' entry, chosen from 95 submittals, was one of eleven projects to be honored. The international jury included several principals of design firms, a special assistant to the Governor of Maryland, the director of the Canadian Centre for Architecture in Montreal, a professor of sculpture, and a senior editor of an architecture magazine. Their judging criteria took into account a project's relationship to the water, design originality and harmony, civic contribution, educational impact, and environmental sensitivity. Categories included artistic and cultural projects, the working waterfront, environmental enhancement, parks and recreation, and mixed-use commercial undertakings.

The jury praised the Harmon Meadow restoration effort as a major mitigation project, involving 158 acres of tidal wetlands. It was interested to see how such a large-scale attempt at introducing a more productive vegetation to a large tract of land in an urban area would fare. The jury was also impressed with the monitoring that continues to be undertaken to record the success of the transformation. It suggested that TAMS develop a comprehensive public education program

Continued on page 3

Above: The Harmon Meadow wetland mitigation site with the Manhattan skyline in the background

In This Issue

Harmon Meadow Restoration Wins Waterfront Award

A Round-Up of Projects Being Worked On In TAMS' Chicago, Raleigh, and SATL Offices

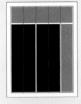

BEFORE: TAMS is built on a 5-column grid. Each text column spans two grid columns; the odd column on the outside is for pictures, captions, and other stuff (here, the contents). Coarse laser printer copy is used as final output; blue ink is added on press for accents.

October 2004

PRODUCED MONTHLY FOR THE EMPLOYEES OF TAMS CONSULTANTS, INC.

HARMON MEADOW WETLANDS RESTORATION WINS HONOR AWARD

Jury Gives Restoration High Praise

THE HARMON MEADOW WETLAND MITIGATION SITE WITH THE MANHATTAN SKYLINE IN THE BACKGROUND

The Harmon Meadow Wetlands Restoration, TAMS' entry in the 2004 Excellence on the Waterfront Award Competition, received an Honor Award at the Waterfront Center's national conference this month. Martin Gold, Hartz Mountain Industries' Director of Planning and Marketing, accepted the award on behalf of TAMS and Hartz Mountain. TAMS Corporate Vice President G. Barrie Heinzenknecht also attended the award presentation and the Waterfront Center conference.

TAMS' entry, chosen from 95 submittals, was one of eleven projects to be honored. The international jury included several principals of design firms, a special assistant to the Governor of Maryland, the director of the Canadian Centre for Architecture in Montreal, a professor of sculpture, and a senior editor of an architecture magazine. Judging criteria took into account a project's relationship to the water, design originality and harmony, civic contribution, educational impact, and environmental sensitivity. Categories included artistic and cultural projects, the working waterfront, environmental enhancement, parks and recreation, and mixed-use commercial undertakings.

The jury praised the Harmon Meadow restoration effort as a major mitigation project, involving 158 acres of tidal wetlands. It was interested to see how such a large-scale attempt at introducing a more productive vegetation to a large tract of land in an urban area would fare.

A page must have a center of focus from which the reader can move. Focus is created through the use of visual contrasts; for example, large to small, dark to light, round to square, many to few, and so on. Here, the designer has laid out a balanced page, yet the result is bland and difficult to read. Why? Everything looks the same! The name, calendar, contents, headlines, and text are so similar in size, style, and weight—and the white space is so uniformly distributed—that the information is effectively masked.

With nothing to attract his eye, the casual reader will turn away. Worse, however, is that the more resolute reader can't tell what's important—or even where to start—without picking through everything himself. Yet the same blandness that makes the page hard to read also makes it appear uninteresting—that is, not worth the trouble.

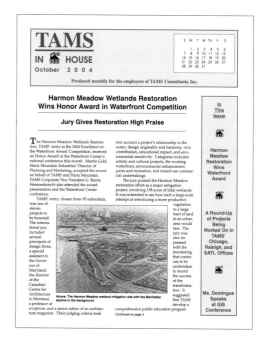

Use visual contrasts to give the reader a focal point

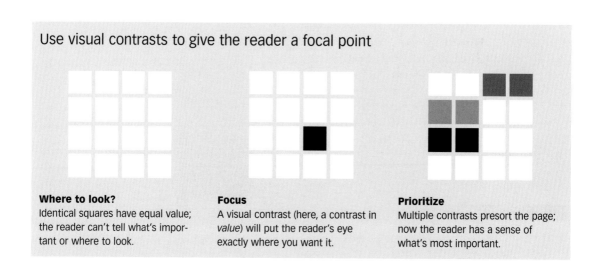

Where to look?
Identical squares have equal value; the reader can't tell what's important or where to look.

Focus
A visual contrast (here, a contrast in *value*) will put the reader's eye exactly where you want it.

Prioritize
Multiple contrasts presort the page; now the reader has a sense of what's most important.

2 Artwork must be attractive

An illustration of any kind sends a powerful message, but you might think of it as a guided—or, more often, unguided—missile. In this case, TAMS is an impersonal, multi-national corporation that the designer tried to warm up by picturing home and hearth. The designer's intent was good, but the result illustrates the heartbreak of clip art. This little house merely looks grade-schoolish, like an escapee from a Monopoly board.

Using artwork to stir a specific feeling—in this case, *warm* and *cared for*—is an extremely difficult undertaking that's best left to the truly artistic. The rest of us should seek a non-illustrative solution in type, shapes, tone values, and so forth. An artistic attempt that falls short will look dumb (or cheap) and is misleading.

The most common error with artwork is that of illustrating a word literally. Here, for example, TAMS IN HOUSE has been illustrated with a house, yet the company, an engineering and environmental planning firm, has nothing to do with houses. Artwork sends a separate message; it should complement, not duplicate, the words.

3 Graphics must be purposeful

A calendar is a very effective graphic device that helps the reader visualize dates by placing them in a familiar context. The unmarked calendar at right, however, conveys no information the reader doesn't already have. Its presence, therefore, adds visual "noise" (anything that draws the eye uselessly) that disturbs communication.

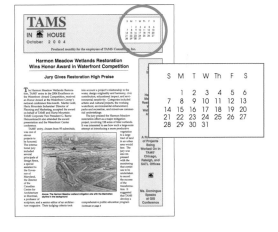

A calendar of important dates can be awkward to construct. Unless it is large (and therefore unsightly), each square is too small for text. Solution? For a small calendar, use oversize text boxes for key dates; add weekend dates for reference; and disregard all other dates. Contrasts add clarity: Note how dark labels clearly stand out.

4   Craftsmanship says it all

Craftsmanship is attention to detail: uniform spacing, alignment of columns, and other particulars like that. Craftsmanship is different from style; it is the fit and finish. A homely but well-crafted page is more professional than a flashy design, poorly built. Some clues:

The eye is quietly disturbed by misalignments, which occur often between captions and text. Adjust carefully.

When used to start a story, an initial capital should be big enough to be seen (try about four times the text size) and for the neatest appearance should align with the baseline of its adjacent text.

The letter *T* is trickier than some. Note how the remainder of the first word tucks tight against it. (The two elements are part of the same word and should be spaced as such.)

Much better!

---

5   Design for the reader

There's a reason the most honored (and widely read) publications are not fashioned in hot, trendy styles: It's because they're designed for the reader, not the artist.

To a reader, words are paramount. A simple page that's a pleasure to read will be perceived as better designed than a more sophisticated page that isn't. When the goal is communication, who else is better qualified to judge?

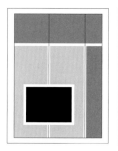 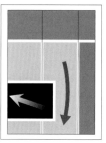

BEFORE   **AFTER**

Details count. Here the designer, in search of a balanced page, centered a photo across two text columns. The result? Extremely narrow passages aside the photo makes reading awkward. A simple alternative was to move the photo to the left margin and up, permitting adequate text to the right and beneath.

The nameplate sets the tone

Nothing sets the tone of a newsletter more certainly than the nameplate. A natural focal point, it is read first and judged instantly. To design a multiword nameplate from scratch, start with type only. Draw the reader's eye with contrasts in size, style, and color. In this way, the words can interact without competing. The greater the contrasts, the quicker you'll start seeing results.

Extremely heavy Futura Extra Bold contrasts sharply with Helvetica Neue Thin, which pulls the eye for a double take. Contrasting colors (white on black) amplify the effect.

Gray (70%) on black permits white type to span the nameplate; black box provides definition and visual "muscle" to attract the eye.

6 | Never point out the obvious

No, no, no, never, never, never. Here, the designer was restricted by the odd column of the 5-column grid and chose to fill the space with a table of contents. Superfluous to this three-article newsletter, its first entry is the adjacent front-page story!

Such a move may seem merely silly, but it can be fatal to the credibility of the editor. How? By pointing out what's obvious, especially in such a prominent space, the newsletter is slighting the reader's intelligence. It instantly becomes a frame of reference; the reader will approach other articles with the silent suspicion that they are equally trivial.

Especially harsh is that this effect is unseen. The reader will rarely be aware of her decision, yet the struggling editor will soon be left wondering why no one is taking her hard work seriously.

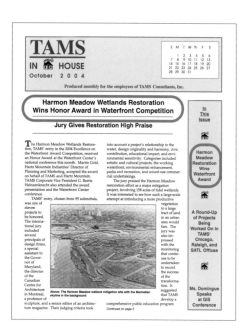

Advanced as it is, the computer has neither eyes nor aesthetic judgment, so don't rely on "auto" for everything. An example:

stries' Director of ███████tion, educational im-
ng, accepted the award ████pact, and environ-
1 Hartz Mountain. ████mental sensitivity.
President G. Barrie ████Categories included
tended the award ████artistic and cultural
Waterfront Center ████projects, the working

BEFORE: 1p6 margin, 3-pica hyphenation zone

v Wetlands Restoration, ████into account a
xcellence on the Water- ████project's relationship
ion, received an Honor ████to the water, design
national conference this ████originality and har-
in Industries' Director ████mony, civic contribu-
ted the award on behalf ████tion, educational im-

AFTER: 0p11 margin, 0-pica hyphenation zone

How ragged is ragged?

Text set ragged right and flush left can leave unexpectedly wide and awkward margins if it is just plopped into place. If your program does not fix the problem automatically and you want a 1½-pica margin, set the space between columns to 1 pica (or even less). In a busy newsletter, it helps to set the *Hyphenation zone* to 0, which forces words as close as possible to the margin before breaking.

Mark Twain said it best: "I'd have written you a shorter letter but I didn't have the time." Newsletters differ on this matter; some topics are so compelling they could be handwritten on Kleenex and still be read. Most, however, are not. Remember, 300-page magazines are routinely perused and tossed aside.

No matter how skilled the designer, a page that's jammed with text will not be read. Your first goal, therefore, is to make your pages *approachable*. This is generally done with pictures (they say lots) and open space, which acts just like an open door.

You say you have five pages of editorial to stuff into four? Try this: Cut it in half, then again. And when you can't cut any more, cut it in half again. If there's nothing left, there was nothing to begin with.

Page 1 makeover has less copy than the original yet is likelier to be read. Why? Noncontributing elements (calendar and contents) have been removed. Disruptive text wraps are gone. The photo is now central. Contrasting styles separate headline and deckhead for clarity. Open space (note the caption) is simply more approachable.

BEFORE: An asymmetrical 5-column grid requires too deft a touch to be practical—the empty outside column is just too wide (a better alternative is seven columns). A clean, three-column page (**After**) is built atop six columns and is much more forgiving. Note that headlines on facing pages are redundant (1); at a glance, right-page text seems like the start of a new article rather than the end.

Headline and graphic are deceptive: They look like a new story rather than a continuation of the cover story (2). Readers will figure it out but they shouldn't have to.

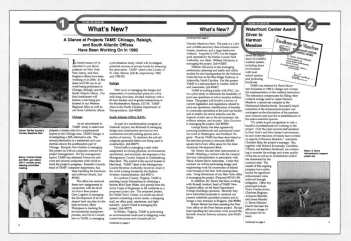

PAGES 2 AND 3 BEFORE

AFTER: White space serves as a stage. It spans the gutter and cleanly unites the two parts of the *What's New?* section. The *jump head* is now proportionate to its importance.

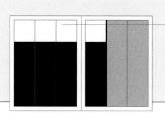

PAGES 2 AND 3 AFTER

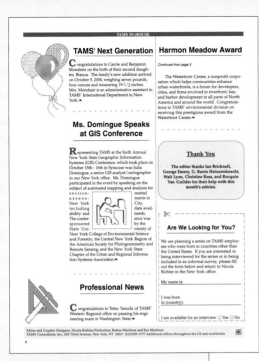

PAGE 4 BEFORE

BEFORE: TAMS' "personal" page is its most read. Why? Because people are most naturally interested in other people. It is no coincidence, however, that this is also the one page where homemade clip art and the *look-who-just-had-a-baby* articles harmonize. The page is exactly what it appears to be.

Even so, the clip art is plainly low grade: Its use lowers the credibility of the organization. Moral: Sometimes using no artwork is a better decision than using poor artwork, as illustrated here.

AFTER: The makeover abandons artwork entirely in favor of splashy typography. It is not an easy solution (this effort took six tries), but note how sharp contrasts in type size, style, and color (just black and white) draw the eye briskly from item to item. Note, too, that no two settings are alike. This tells the reader that each is a different kind of item.

Ms. Domingue Speaks at GIS Conference

Representing TAMS at the Sixth Annual New York State Geographic Information Systems (GIS) Conference, which took place on October 15th–16th in Syracuse was Julia Domingue, a senior GIS analyst/cartographer in our New York office. Ms. Domingue participated in the event by speaking on the subject of automated mapping and analysis for environmental assessments in New York City, including data availability and needs. The conference was sponsored by the State University of New York College of Environmental Science and Forestry, the Central New York Region of the American Society for Photogrammetry and Remote Sensing, and the New York State Chapter of the Urban and Regional Information Systems Association.

THANK YOU
THE EDITOR THANKS IAN BRICKNELL, GEORGE EMERY, G. BARRIE HEINZENKNECHT, WALT LYON, CHRISTINE ROSS, AND ROCQUIN VAN GUILDER FOR THEIR HELP WITH THIS MONTH'S ARTICLES.

TAMS' *Next Generation*

Congratulations to Carole and Benjamin Mondesir on the birth of their second daughter, Bianca. The family's new addition arrived on October 5, 2004, weighing seven pounds, four ounces and measuring 19½ inches. Mrs. Mondesir is an administrative assistant in TAMS' International Department in New York.

Professional News

Congratulations...
to Tetsu Yasuda of TAMS' Western Regional office on passing his engineering exam in Washington State.

TAMS In House

EDITOR AND GRAPHIC DESIGNER
Nicola Richter

PRODUCTION
Ruben Martinez and Ray Martinez

TAMS Consultants, Inc.
655 Third Avenue
New York, NY 10017
(212) 555-1777

Additional offices throughout the US and worldwide.

Are We Looking for You?

We are planning a series on TAMS employees who were born in countries other than the United States. If you are interested in being interviewed for the series or in being included in an informal survey, please fill out the form below and return to Nicola Richter in the New York office.

My name is: _____

I was born
in (country): _____

I am available for an interview ☐ Yes ☐ No

PAGE 4 AFTER

The reader will move confidently through a publication if its typography establishes a definite hierarchy, thereby making it clear what he or she is about to read. Hierarchy is most easily created with typographic contrasts.

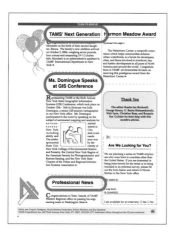

TAMS' Next Generation
Professional News
Ms. Domingue Speaks
at GIS Conference

You can't tell these heads apart: Identically set in Helvetica Bold, they give the reader no clue that they are different kinds of information.

TAMS' NEXT GENERATION
PROFESSIONAL NEWS

Ms. Domingue Speaks
at GIS Conference

The same words set in contrasting sizes, styles, and colors. It's clear at a glance which are *standing heads* (regularly published pieces) and which is a story headline.

Cropping almost always improves a photograph

Back to the future
In the photographer's eye was a fine sense of history—the vice president in person at an award-winning project site—but what's actually recorded is a tiny man, ankle-deep in gray grass.

Zoom in on the subject
Cropping brings the vice president into view; it's how a designer says, "Look here." Reflect or flop the photo so that the man faces into the layout, holding the reader's eye to the page. Be careful, though: Not everything works when it is backward (text, for example).

Motion adds vigor
You'll need retouching software to take this step, but the reader now has something in common with the VP: His windy blueprints have emerged into our world.

What typefaces go together? Here's how to mix and match.

Typeface combinations

Do you really need more than the fonts that came with your printer? No, the basics are quite good. But if you do want to invest in a type library, where do you start?

Start by identifying type *categories:* These five groups cover most of the characteristics that differentiate one font from another.

And your purchase plan? Start by adding one thing that standard printer fonts *don't* provide: a sans serif font with really bold bolds. Then to round out your collection, add one serif font from each group.

When combining serif and sans serif text fonts, try to match characteristics of *form*, such as wide, round shapes or narrow, vertical ones; and details of *proportion*, such as large x-height letters versus small x-height.

Try to match x-heights of fonts that appear side by side—even if you must use different point sizes. Or, you can exaggerate their differences by making one font at least two point sizes bigger—or a whole lot bolder—than the other.

OLDSTYLE FACES look great when combined with Humanist style sans serifs—like Gill Sans or Frutiger—because they share similarly shaped characteristics, proportions, and weight stresses.

This run-in head is 7-point Frutiger Ultra Black, a Humanist sans serif, shown here with 9-point Cochin, an Oldstyle font, and *Cochin Italic*, one of the most *unusual* and *beautiful* italics. Note that we've used two different point sizes but that we've made the x-heights of the two fonts match.

This run-in head is 7-point Gill Sans Extra Bold, also a Humanist sans serif, shown here with 8.5-point Goudy, another Oldstyle body text, and *Goudy Italic*, another very *beautiful* and *legible italic* font. Note that the two fonts at left share a similar horizontal character form, while these two share slightly more vertical and rounded letterforms.

TRANSITIONAL FONTS have more mechanical, geometric forms and measurements than the Oldstyles, and look best combined with bold geometric sans serif fonts like the Futura or Univers families.

Futura, a geometric font with a lot of weight variations like this 7.5-point Condensed Extra Bold, looks great with a *Transitional* font like this 8-point Times Ten, which is a variation on the classic Times font that came with your laser printer. They both share slightly vertical letterform shapes and crisp, geometric distribution of weight.

This head is 7-point Univers Black 75, shown here with 8-point New Baskerville, another Transitional body text with a *lovely italic*. The Univers family of geometric sans serifs, like Futura, has a wide choice of weights and widths. Again, we've combined fonts that have similar letterforms and character widths, and matched x-heights.

MODERN FONTS have even more refined geometric forms and exaggerated thicks and thins than the Transitionals. They combine well with geometric sans serifs like Futura.

Another geometric sans serif font, this 6.5-point Futura Extra Bold looks great matched with a Modern font like this 8.5-point Bauer Bodoni. They both share wide, rounded letterform shapes and balanced distribution of weight. Futura's exaggerated weight sets off the Bodoni's high-contrast thick/thin nicely.

This head is 7.5-point Futura Heavy with 8.5-point De Vinne, another Modern face like Bodoni, but one that has much less thick/thin contrast. The De Vinne is so light that it doesn't need a very bold weight sans serif with it. It also has a narrower shape that the Futura Heavy matches better than the wider Futuras Bold or Extra Bold.

SLAB SERIF, OR EGYPTIAN, FONTS that were developed for display work in the 19th century share the proportions—including larger x-height—of the moderns, but have less thick/thin contrast.

Slab serifs like this 7.5-point Memphis Extra Bold can be used as heads when combined with any simple, sans serif body type that shares their general proportions, like this 8-point Avenir Roman. This reverses the usual habit of using serifs for body and sans serifs for heads, and gives a casual, airy look.

This combination of 7.5-point Franklin Gothic Heavy and 8-point Century Expanded, an Egyptian face, is a friendly mix. The Century family—Schoolbook, Expanded and Oldstyle—are classic news fonts that look great with any of the grotesque sans serifs, like Franklin or News Gothic.

SANS SERIF FONTS also have a large x-height proportion and modern forms, but even stroke weight distribution. Families often provide a wide range of widths and weights.

This 7-point Helvetica Black shows the wide range of weights available with a sans serif font family. Using extreme contrasts of weight, such as **Black**, above, and this 8-point Helvetica Light, makes a more elegant combination than these **bold** and medium weights, which have less contrast of weight.

Sans serif fonts, like this 7.5-point Helvetica, can be a low-key background against which to feature *Scripts, like this 8-point Kaufmann Bold*, and other decorative fonts that need a simple background, like this **5.5-point Blackoak**, a replica of an old wood type poster display font from the 1800s.

Design a newsletter that's elegantly tall. | By Chuck Green

Head and shoulders above the rest

Consider this stately newsletter design, a format that simply folds a letter-size sheet lengthwise. Its tall front panel looks like the cover of a magazine or brochure, which gives the newsletter the opportunity to show well as a stylish pass-along piece. Open, its pages combine into a more traditional-looking, two-column newsletter. The format is excellent for long, narrative-style articles.

To work with *tall*, you want to think tall. Think subjects that are *towering, elevated, grand*. It's a format for trees, mountains, skyscrapers. Tall can convey power, accomplishment, heavenly things. It can show distance and depth. Other tall words:

- High, lofty, magnificent

- Reach up and touch the sky

- Stars, skies, planes, stairs, clouds, lightning, towers, floating, balloons, far off, future.

Let's have a look.

A letter-size sheet folded lengthwise yields a stately page especially suitable for a narrative-style newsletter. Sixteen pages are four sheets folded as shown and stapled.

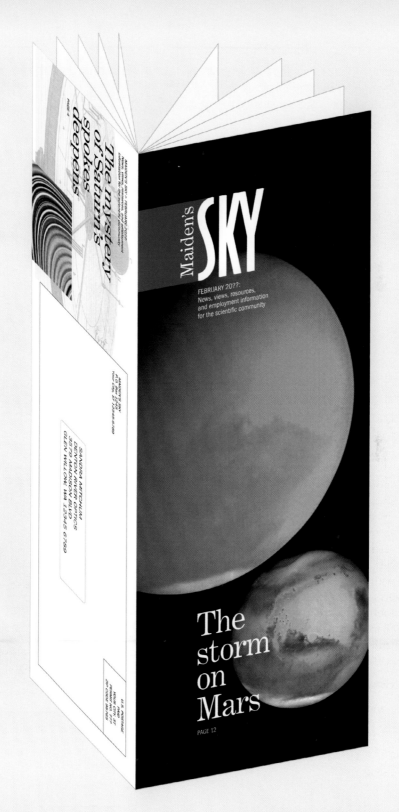

Build two page grids, one for text pages, the other for headline pages. See the shaded box to the right for dimensions in inches.

A narrative-style newsletter needs a great storytelling typeface. Century Expanded, full of texture and history, is the choice for both text and headlines. Franklin Gothic Book Condensed is an ideal compliment for lists, details, and other small accents.

Document setup
Text pages: Top: 1", Outside: ¼", Inside: ½", Bottom: ⅜"
Headline pages: Top: 1", Outside: 1", Inside: ½", Bottom: ⅜"

Aa

CENTURY EXPANDED

Bb

FRANKLIN GOTHIC BOOK CONDENSED

Headline page
Note the wide left margin.

MAIDEN'S SKY > FEBRUARY 20??
News, views, resources, and employment
information for the scientific community

Standby. The "money moments" before launch.

BY TAMRA EXAMPLE

Lorem ipsum dolor sit amet, consectetuer adipiscing elit, sed diam nonummy nibh euismod tincidunt ut laoreet dolore magna aliquam erat volutpat. Ut wisi enim ad minim veniam, quis nostrud exerci tation ullam corper suscipit lobortis nisl ut aliquip ex ea commodo consequat. Duis autem vel eum iriure dolor in hendrerit in vulputate velit esse molestie consequat. continued on page 3

Text page

The headline, long lead-in (red, **4**) and photo captions give the opportunity to tell your story in shorter bites with differing emphasis, or to tell mini-stories that complement the main one, or both. Either way, the short stories are reader-friendly and always welcome.

Type specs
1, **3**, **5** Franklin Gothic Book Condensed 8/9; **2** Century Expanded 32/30; **4** Century Expanded Italic 14/16; **6** Century Expanded 10/12.

Typography has a readable, touchable texture

Type plays a key role in this newsletter and gets its appeal from a careful blend of sizes and styles. Ragged right margins feel organic, not blocky.

① MAIDEN'S SKY > FEBRUARY 20??
News, views, resources, and employment
information for the scientific community

② The mystery of Saturn's spokes deepens

③ BY ROBIN EXAMPLE

④ *Lorem ipsum dolor sit amet, consectetuer adipiscing elit, sed diam nonummy nibh euismod tincidunt ut laoreet dolore magna aliquam erat volutpat. Ut wisi enim ad minim veniam, quis nostrud exerci tation ullam corper suscipit lobortis nisl ut aliquip ex ea commodo consequat. Duis autem vel eum iriure dolor in hendrerit in vulputate velit esse molestie consequat.*

⑤ Lorem ipsum dolor sit amet, consectetuer adipiscing elit, sed diam nonummy nibh euismod tincidunt

Dolor sit amet, consectetuer adipiscing elit, sed diam nonummy nibh euismod tincidunt ut laoreet dolore

⑥ Lorem ipsum dolor sit amet, consectetuer adipiscing elit, sed diam nonummy nibh euismod tincidunt ut laoreet dolore magna aliquam erat volutpat. Ut wisi enim ad minim veniam, quis nostrud exerci tation ullam corper suscipit lobortis nisl ut aliquip ex ea commodo consequat. Duis autem vel eum iriure dolor in hendrerit in vulputate velit esse molestie consequat, vel illum dolore eu feugiat nulla facilisis at vero eros et accumsan et iusto odio dignissim qui blandit praesent luptatum zzril delenit augue duis dolore te feugait nulla facilisi.
Lorem ipsum dolor sit amet, consectetuer adipiscing elit, sed diam nonummy nibh euismod tincidunt ut laoreet dolore magna aliquam erat volutpat. Ut wisi enim ad minim veniam, quis nostrud exerci tation ullamcorper suscipit lobortis nisl ut aliquip ex ea commodo consequat. Duis autem vel eum iriure dolor in hendrerit in vulputate velit esse molestie consequat, vel illum dolore eu feugiat nulla facilisis at vero eros et Nam liber tempor cum soluta nobis eleifend option congue nihil imperdiet doming id quod mazim placerat facer possim assum.
Lorem ipsum dolor sit amet, consectetuer adipiscing elit, sed diam nonummy nibh euismod tincidunt ut laoreet dolore magna aliquam erat volutpat. Ut wisi enim ad minim veniam, quis nostrud exerci tation ullamcorper suscipit lobortis nisl ut aliquip ex ea commodo consequat. Lorem ipsum dolor sit amet, consectetuer adipiscing elit, sed diam nonummy nibh euismod tincidunt ut laoreet dolore erat volutpat. Sed diam nonummy nibh euismod tincidunt ut laoreet dolore magna aliquam erat volutpat. Ut wisi enim ad minim veniam, quis nostrud exerci tation ullam corper suscipit lobortis nisl ut aliquip ex ea commodo consequat. Duis autem vel eum iriure dolor.

Contact Robin Example: 987 654 3210;
name@emailaddressz.com; More: http://www.yourwebaddressz.com/
articles/storyname.htm

5

A secondary visual element—in this case, a series of beautifully complex antique scientific diagrams and illustrations—adds a rich visual theme and gives the newsletter real depth. Note that their page-wide square format anchors all headline pages. The images create a subtle visual connection from page to page.

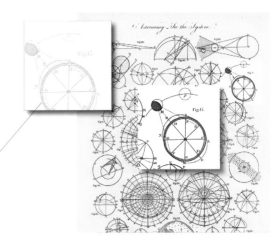

Illustrations are easily cropped from a larger image; the horizontal lines are added in Photoshop.

Design a tall nameplate

A tall format needs a tall name! Raleigh Gothic Medium Condensed complements the shape of the page. In Adobe Illustrator, scale your text to just beyond the edge of a rectangle (1), change it to outlines, use the Divide tool to cookie-cut the word out of the background (2), then apply colors (3). Have a longer name? Try a variation on the theme (4) using a colored box to encapsulate the subtitle.

The contents page is where your newsletter really gets started. For continuity, repeat the cover nameplate (black here instead of white), then list all the small but permanent information—issue date and subtitle, contents, contact information, primary staff, masthead, copyright, and so on.

MAIDEN'S SKY > FEBRUARY 20??
News, views, resources, and employment information for the scientific community

Maiden's **SKY**

INSIDE	Page
Article title one ipsum dolor sit amet	Cover
Article title two dolor sit amet	2
Article title three sit amet	2
Article title four ipsum dolor sit amet	3
Article title five ipsum	3
Article title six ipsum dolor	4
Article title seven ipsum dolor sit amet	4
Article title eight dolor sit amet	5
Article title nine ipsum sit amet	5
Article title ten ipsum dolor amet	6
Article title eleven ipsum dolor sit	6
Article title twelve dolor sit amet	6
Article title thirteen ipsum sit amet	7
Article title fourteen ipsum dolor	8

3028 Example Road, P.O. Box 1245
Your City, ST 12345-6789
987 654 3210
987 654 3210 Fax
info@emailaddressz.com

EXECUTIVE DIRECTOR
Sarah Example
987 654 3210
name@emailaddressz.com

NEWSLETTER EDITOR
Charles Example
987 654 3210
name@emailaddressz.com

NEWSLETTER NAME (ISSN #1234-5678), FEBRUARY 20??, Volume One, Number Five, Published by Organization's Name, 3028 Example Road, Your City, ST 12345-6789. $12/yr. POSTMASTER: Send address changes to Publication Name, 3028 Example Road, Your City, ST 12345-6789. Copyright 20?? by Organization's Name. All rights reserved. Legal Disclaimer. Copyright Clearance Center.

From the editor: Stormy weather

Lorem ipsum dolor sit amet, consectetuer adipiscing elit, sed diam nonummy nibh euismod tincidunt ut laoreet dolore magna aliquam erat volutpat. Ut wisi enim ad minim veniam, quis nostrud exerci tation ullam corper suscipit lobortis nisl ut aliquip ex ea commodo consequat. Duis autem vel eum iriure dolor in hendrerit in vulputate velit esse molestie consequat, vel illum dolore eu feugiat nulla facilisis at vero eros et accumsan et iusto odio dignissim qui blandit praesent luptatum zzril delenit augue duis dolore te feugait nulla facilisi.

Lorem ipsum dolor sit amet, consectetuer adipiscing elit, sed diam nonummy nibh euismod tincidunt ut laoreet dolore magna aliquam erat volutpat. Ut wisi enim ad minim veniam, quis nostrud exerci tation ullamcorper suscipit lobortis nisl ut aliquip ex ea commodo consequat. Duis autem vel eum iriure dolor in hendrerit in vulputate velit esse molestie consequat, vel illum dolore eu feugiat nulla facilisis at vero eros et Nam liber tempor cum soluta nobis eleifend option congue nihil imperdiet doming id quod mazim placerat facer possim assum.

Lorem ipsum dolor sit amet, consectetuer adipiscing elit, sed diam nonummy nibh euismod tincidunt ut laoreet dolore magna aliquam erat volutpat. Ut wisi enim ad minim veniam, quis nostrud exerci tation ullamcorper suscipit lobortis nisl ut aliquip ex ea commodo consequat. Lorem ipsum dolor sit amet, consectetuer adipiscing elit, sed diam nonummy nibh euismod tincidunt ut laoreet dolore erat volutpat. Sed diam nonummy nibh euismod tincidunt ut laoreet dolore magna aliquam erat volutpat. Ut wisi enim ad minim veniam, quis nostrud exerci tation ullam corper suscipit lobortis nisl ut aliquip ex ea commodo consequat. Duis autem vel eum iriure dolor in hendrerit in vulputate velit esse molestie consequat, vel illum dolore eu feugiat nulla facilisis at vero eros et accumsan et iusto odio dignissim qui blandit praesent luptatum zzril delenit augue duis dolore te feugait nulla facilisi.

Contact Bailey Example: 987 654 3210; name@emailaddressz.com; More: http://www.yourwebaddressz.com/articles/storyname.htm

3

Keep visual interest moving through your pages by staggering the illustrations. Since form must follow function, you won't always get an artistic balance, but try for it; what you want to avoid in any case are unrelieved acres of gray text.

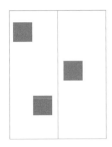

Ut wisi enim ad minim veniam, quis nostrud exerci tation ullam corper suscipit lobortis nisl ut aliquip ex ea commodo consequat. Duis autem vel eum iriure dolor in hendrerit in vulputate velit esse molestie consequat, vel illum dolore eu feugiat nulla facilisis at vero eros et accumsan et iusto odio dignissim qui blandit praesent luptatum zzril delenit augue duis dolore te feugait nulla facilisi.

Lorem ipsum dolor sit amet, consectetuer adipiscing elit, sed diam nonummy nibh euismod tincidunt ut laoreet dolore magna aliquam erat volutpat. Ut wisi enim ad minim veniam, quis nostrud exerci tation ullamcorper suscipit lobortis nisl ut aliquip ex ea commodo consequat. Duis autem vel eum iriure dolor in hendrerit in vulputate velit esse molestie consequat, vel illum dolore eu feugiat nulla facilisis at vero eros et Nam liber tempor cum soluta nobis eleifend option congue nihil imperdiet doming id quod mazim placerat facer possim assum.

Lorem ipsum dolor sit amet, consectetuer adipiscing elit, sed diam nonummy nibh euismod tincidunt ut laoreet dolore magna aliquam erat volutpat. Ut wisi enim ad minim veniam, quis nostrud exerci tation ullamcorper suscipit lobortis nisl ut aliquip ex ea commodo consequat. Lorem ipsum dolor sit amet, consectetuer adipiscing elit, sed diam nonummy nibh euismod tincidunt ut laoreet dolore erat volutpat. Sed diam nonummy nibh euismod tincidunt ut laoreet dolore magna aliquam erat volutpat. Ut wisi enim ad minim veniam, quis nostrud exerci tation ullam corper suscipit lobortis nisl ut aliquip ex ea commodo consequat. Lorem ipsum dolor sit amet, consectetuer adipiscing elit, sed diam nonummy nibh euismod tincidunt ut laoreet dolore magna aliquam erat volutpat. Ut wisi enim ad minim veniam, quis nostrud exerci tation

Dolor sit amet, consectetuer adipiscing elit, sed diam nonummy nibh euismod

ullam corper suscipit lobortis nisl ut aliquip ex ea commodo consequat. Duis autem vel eum iriure dolor in hendrerit in vulputate velit esse molestie consequat, vel illum dolore eu feugiat nulla facilisis at vero eros et accumsan et iusto odio dignissim qui blandit praesent.

Lorem ipsum dolor sit amet, consectetuer adipiscing elit, sed diam nonummy nibh euismod tincidunt ut laoreet dolore magna aliquam erat volutpat. Ut wisi enim ad minim veniam, quis nostrud exerci tation ullamcorper suscipit lobortis nisl ut aliquip ex ea commodo consequat. Duis autem vel eum iriure dolor in hendrerit in vulputate velit esse molestie consequat, vel illum dolore eu feugiat nulla facilisis at vero eros et Nam liber tempor cum soluta nobiserat eleifend option congue nihil imperdiet doming id quod mazim placerat facer possim assum.

Lorem ipsum dolor sit amet, consectetuer aliquam adipiscing elit, sed diam nonummy nibh euismod dolore tincidunt ut laoreet dolore magna aliquam erat erat volutpat. Ut wisi enim ad minim veniam, quis nostrud exerci tation ullamcorper suscipit lobortis nisl ut aliquip ex ea commodo consequat. Lorem ipsum dolor sit amet, consectetuer adipiscing elit, sed diam

Lorem ipsum dolor sit amet, consectetuer adipiscing elit, sed diam nonummy nibh euismod tincidunt ut

nonummy nibh euismod tincidunt ut laoreet nulla dolore erat volutpat. wisi enim ad minim feug veniam, quis nostrud exerci tation ullamcorper suscipit lobortis nisl ut aliquip excom tincidunter consequat. Duis autem vel eum iriure dolor hendrerit in vulputate velit esse molestie consequat, vel illum dolore eu feugiat nulla facilisis at vero eros et Nam liber tempor cum soluta nobis eleifend option congue nihil imperdiet doming id quod mazim placerat facer possim assum.

Lorem ipsum dolor sit amet, consectetuer magna adipiscing elit, sed diam nonummy nibh euismod tincidunt ut laoreet dolore magna aliquam erat volutpat. Ut wisi enim ad minim veniam, quis nostrud exerci tation ullamcorper suscipit lobortis nisl ut aliquip ex ea commodo consequat. Lorem ipsum dolor sit amet, consectetuer adipiscing elit, sed diam nonummy nibh euismod tincidunt ut laoreet dolore erat volutpat. Sed diam nonummy nibh euismod tincidunt ut laoreet dolore magna aliquam erat volutpat. Ut wisi enim ad minim veniam, quis nostrud exerci tation ullam corper suscipit lobortis nisl ut aliquip ex ea commodo consequat.

Contact Tamra Example: 987 654 3210; name@emailaddressz.com; More: http://www.yourwebaddressz.com/articles/storyname.htm

14

15

Many readers see the back of your newsletter first, so start the issue right there with a teaser. Repeat the story title and an image from the inside (same fonts and format; note here the repeating squares) to summarize and tantalize.

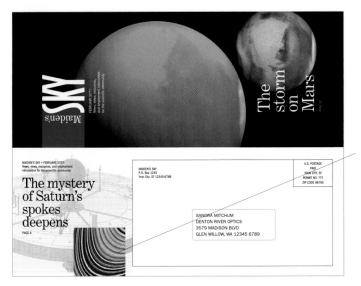

Use squares
Note throughout that images are either square (half- or full-page wide) or full page; there is no in-between shape.

Make it easy to get in touch

Do you want readers to contact you? Make it easy; include on *every page* the author's name, phone number, e-mail address, and—if you have a companion Web site—a link to more information about the article's subject. Note here that a square icon gives the contact block more visibility.

Eye-catching and fun to read, this unusual newsletter is made of boxes.

Lively newsletter puts everyone on stage!

This newsletter has to please a lot of people. Published by a health care group, the publication is distributed to doctors, medical offices, referral services, and the residents of the company's many convalescent homes and their families. It is an important marketing tool that represents the whole organization, but it is written especially for the benefit of its patients and the employees who care for them.

Its emphasis is on people. It includes *Yes, We Can!*, a program that highlights extra-special service by outstanding caregivers; feature articles about residents; and a regular birthday and personal landmark column. The idea is to get everyone involved. It includes medical news and even a word puzzle.

That's a lot of material and photos, and everything changes every issue. So here's the challenge: Design a newsletter in two colors that carries news, letters, columns, and features, one that is punctuated by a dozen *People* magazine-like articles and blurbs. It has to be visually engaging, fun to read, and represent the company in a professional manner. The designer does not have a large art collection. Here's what can be done with such challenges.

BEFORE

BEFORE

Wanted: A newsletter that puts people first

The designer of this newsletter wanted a front page full of people, activity, and exuberance, for which she arranged a splashy head, big photos, and a minimum of copy. To make her type dance, she varied it a lot—stretched it, compressed it, spread it out, overlapped it. But she ran into an intractable problem: Photos, even good ones (which these aren't) are surprisingly poor storytellers. A camera can't hear a laugh or bask in applause or enjoy a twice-told tale. It can't smell cooking or feel the breeze. It records nothing at all but the physical scene—and only a tiny portion of that.

AFTER

What to do?

Exercise some visual choreography. Let's put our photos and the stories that accompany them into dozens of decorative boxes. These boxes—and the inventive embellishments you create for them—will form the visual foundation of the newsletter. This looks great, and instead of a burdensome leading role, our fairly humdrum photos will now play a more appropriate supporting role. Here's how to do all that.

There's a lot of structure beneath this airy make-over. A blocky nameplate sits atop a seven-column grid (**1**); six columns are used for text and photos, while the outer column catches the over-flow. The page is divided horizontally into two zones, roughly one third on top and two-thirds beneath. The top third holds the nameplate and index. The bottom two-thirds form our layout zone (**2**). Into this zone go smaller boxes that contain the articles and photos. The airspace directly beneath the nameplate remains empty.

1

Establish the layout zone

For a light, accessible look, you need a really wide margin. Set guides to form a square around six of the seven columns.

Crisscross two axes

Set guides to mark a pivot around which the stories will be arranged. The pivot is important, but its location is flexible.

Rough in the text

Set text and heads in place around the pivot. This is mainly a visualizing step; note that two skinny columns are treated as one normal one.

Make a dominant story

To anchor the page, make one story BIG. A good way is to double (or so) its type size and leading, then spread it across four columns. Note its now-smaller photo bleeds to the left edge.

Box and balance

The other two stories go in decorative boxes, though type size remains the same. The idea is to now color them for weight (darker is heavier) and arrange them for balance. Bottom photo extends downward past the box and border; the emblem interrupts the empty column. A right-sized box aligns with the top of the adjacent text (right), but is shortened from the bottom for balance.

Note alignment

Boxes are the decorative focal point of this newsletter, and no device could be more versatile. They can shrink, expand, or change shape. They can hold text, photos, or both, and they can be embellished in all kinds of simple ways. It's important, though, that the text—especially the typestyles—remain consistent. This design relies on two type families, a sans serif mainly for heads and flags (**1** and **2**), and a serif mainly for text (**3**).

Wortham's Quest
PAGE 6 Chuck Bumpass and staff captured the coveted Quest for Quality Award by delivering Red Rose service.

Wortham's Quest
PAGE 6 Chuck Bumpass and his staff captured the coveted Quest for Quality Award by delivering Red Rose service.

Contents align neatly with horizontal bars.

Extra-wide text leading adds air; a photo peeks above the border. Bar adds visual weight.

A nameplate based on the corporate logo

It's pretty daring to name your newsletter a whole sentence, so *Care Matters to Everyone* warranted a plucky nameplate. This company has a professionally designed logo, from which a flower is borrowed to give our nameplate a "family resemblance." Here's how it was done.

CHARTWELL GROUP OF HEALTHCARE COMPANIES

1. Set name in caps aligned left on very tight leading. Here it's 82/64.

2. Kern tightly. Normal spacing is meant only for text size; the bigger the words, the tighter they should be set.

3. This is an unsightly overlap that we doctored away in a draw program. Watch for similar distractions.

4. Enlarge initial letters 20 percent (or so). Use Baseline shift to pump lower letter down flush with the tops.

5. Reverse from dark green. Unequal length words left room for the flower. Is your long word on top? Put the graphic on the bottom.

6. We traced the flower and, to host it, added a decorative arch. Fat-stroked petals are tints of black (10 and 30 percent); leaves are tints of green (50 and 75 percent), dark enough to work behind the type.

7. Small descriptive words in matching caps were spaced out, then colored faint tints of green and black. White words are thinly shadowed in black. A hairline top edge completes the job.

This is *Care Matters'* people section; it acknowledges special employees and interesting residents, and is one of its most popular features. A section like this typically contains several stories under one heading. You want your design to make each of them stand out, yet look like they belong together. It should have similarity and variety at the same time.

We're doing this here with flexible, decorative boxes. The boxes establish a family resemblance, yet each is unique, distinct from the others. Each story has its own personality and eye-catching appeal.

A box-style layout is an editor's delight. Instead of fading into monotonous columns (**BEFORE**), stories appear shorter, more manageable, and more interesting. And it's easy to fill the space. Boxes can change size, shape, content, and color (or value) to suit the page.

All that's left is for you to decide how to embellish each box. Here are some pointers:

The column trap

When you see blank columns, it's quite natural to want to fill them top to bottom. But this rarely yields the most interesting layouts. Our box-style layout uses columns only as guides, not containers. Note that text and boxes freely span two or even three grid columns.

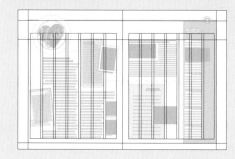

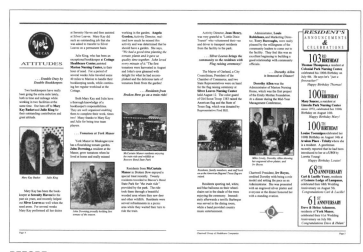

BEFORE

1. A foundation of typographic "glue"

Our first "box" isn't a box at all. It's a page of easy-to-read oversize text that draws attention because of its size and forms the "glue" that holds the layout together. Without this text oozing around and between boxes, they would appear hard-edged and separate. The two text columns span six grid columns. As type gets bigger, its leading should get proportionately tighter. For example, if your normal text is 10/12, set oversize text 15/17, or even 20/22. Note the hairline between columns.

Specs

Headline: 14/16 Frutiger Ultra Black, all caps, align left. **Text:** 14/16 Sabon, align left. **Paragraph specs:** Indents, 1p6 (no indent on lead paragraph); **Paragraph space:** Before, 0p4 (lead paragraph only).

2. The floating-photo box

The trick just looks fun. Photos that float boost people appeal. Green text on green has soft contrast, and it doesn't compete with the photo. The box fits grid columns, but a tilted photo can be an odd size; rules at top and bottom are visual anchors. A lifelike drop shadow adds dimension.

Specs

Run-in headline: 9/10 Frutiger Ultra Black, all caps. **Text:** 8/10 Frutiger Bold, align left. **Type color:** 100 percent green. **Tint background:** 25 percent green. **Lines:** 2-pt. and 60 percent green, align to text. **White photo border:** 0p9 from edge of photo, 100K hairline rule.

AFTER

3. The graduated-fill box

Built the width of two grid columns, then rotated six degrees, this box takes advantage of a fill that graduates from medium to light green. A graduated fill has an appealing natural glow that flat fills do not have. Medium green at the top forms a neutral-value background against which both white and black type show clearly (below left). Light green at the bottom is a fine backdrop for the clip-art locomotive, whose visual weight is offset by the heavy 4-pt. rule on the box's top and right edges. Breaking the border (below right) adds a touch of visual tension.

Note alignment

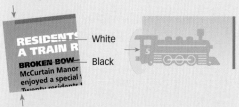

White

Black

Specs

Headline: 10/10 Frutiger Ultra Black, all caps align left. Fill white. **Subhead:** 7/8 Frutiger Ultra Black, all caps. **Text:** 7/8 Frutiger Bold, align left. **Paragraph space:** Before, 0p3. **Tint background:** graduated from 40 to 10 percent green. **Lines:** 4 pt., 60 percent green. **Train:** 30 percent green.

4. The fancy first-letter box

Have a story that's too short? Here's an attractive way to stretch it. The brief text and small photo here occupy one-third of the page. *Justified* text on super-deep leading suggests elegance and formality. Note that the fancy first letter overlaps the box and underprints the text. The headline gets pushed aside but is centered above the dingbat. As a rule, the margin widths and other gaps should be equal to or greater than the line leading.

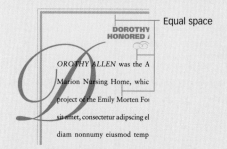

Equal space

Specs

Headline: 8/8 Frutiger Ultra Black, all caps, fill with 50 percent black. **Dingbat:** 20-pt. Adobe Woodtype Ornaments 2, fill 40 percent green. **Initial:** 120/120 Snell Roundhand Script, fill 60 percent green. **Text:** 8/20 Sabon, justified. Note that text overprints the initial. **Tint box:** 5-pt. double rule, 40 percent green, fill with 10 percent green.

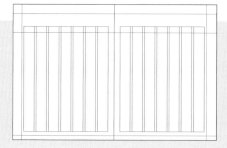

Document setup

Page: Letter, 8½ × 11-inch, tall orientation, double-sided, facing pages; **Margins (in picas):** Inside 3, Outside 6, Top 11, Bottom 5. **Column guides:** 7; space between 1 pica. **Horizontal ruler guides:** 14 and 63 picas from top of the page. **Vertical ruler guides:** 46 on each page measuring from spread center.

5. The wall-to-wall box

This carpet of dark green anchors the entire two-page spread. Such a heavy visual weight is a tool with which you can shift the balance of a space. White type is an appealing contrast, but to ensure readability against the dark background, it is set in a bold, sans-serif style with extra space between lines. The justified column sharply defines the right edge. Note the left edge does not mate with the grid: Doing so would crowd the adjacent stories, so it's been pulled back two picas. The text runs from column six to one pica shy of the left box edge, the same distance as the space between columns.

Specs

Run-in subhead: 15/14 Frutiger Extra Black Condensed, small caps, fill with white. **Text:** 8/14 Frutiger Bold Condensed, justified, fill with white. Extra return between paragraphs. **Tint box:** 40 percent green.

Reversed type is a bold sans serif for maximum readability.

100TH birth...
lestaie son conse...
dolore eu fugiat n...

Left edge of box is 2p0 from the grid line.

Text begins 1p0 from edge of box, the same distance as the space between columns.

Visual imagery gets stronger with repetition. The more frequently a viewer sees your logo, for example, the stronger the connection between it and your product will be. It's a good idea to repeat your imagery from page to page of your newsletter. We've illustrated here the three most common ways:

1. Consistent typography (that is, one or two type families used again and again)

2. Consistent color

3. Recurring graphics—in this case, the ruled border, flower, column headings, and page number below

Specs
Type: ITC Berkeley Oldstyle Bold. Sizes will vary. Enlarge initial letter about 20 percent.

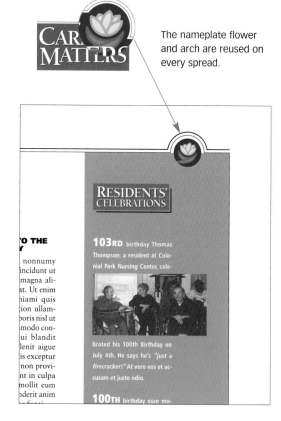

The nameplate flower and arch are reused on every spread.

Two icons from one nameplate

Our picturesque nameplate lends its characteristics to two separate icons that are repeated throughout the newsletter. First, the flower and arch are worked into the border of every spread, in the same—this is important—size, color, and position.

The nameplate's typography is then applied to the column headings. *Typography* means more than just typestyle: It means the *look* of the thing. In this case, first match the typestyle, then set your primary words in all caps, margin to margin (if your word is too short, add space between letters). *Force justify* smaller secondary word(s), above or below (or both). Enlarge the initial letter of the primary word 20 percent (or so), then bump it up or down as before, depending on what line it's on.

Watch for similar "two-fer" opportunities in your newsletters.

Column heads repeat the nameplate's typography.

Mix and match! Tints make two colors look like a dozen

Does your budget permit only two colors? You're not stuck with only flat black and flat green: You can stretch those colors a lot. One of your computer's best assets is its ability to make tints. Add to your palette of black, white, and green nine grays and nine green tints, then mix and match in endless ways—gray on black, green on gray, white on green, and so on. In addition to creating variety, tints are *balancers*—darks are heavy, lights are feathery. If your page is tipping to one side, lighten its tints or add darkness to the other side.

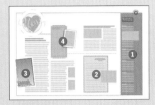

Balance
Tints (plus box size and position) help balance a page: **1** dark, **2** light, and **3** and **4** medium tints keep this spread moving.

Type: 20% green. Drop shadow: 100% black. Box: 70% green. Outer box: 15% black with 100% green stroke.

Type: White. Box: Graduated fill 40% to 10% green. Lines: 100% green and 100% black.

Type: 100% green. Box: 25% green. Lines: 100% green.

Type: 60% green. Box: 10% green with 40% green stroke. Lines: 50% black and 100% black.

Type: White. Box: 40% green.

Type: White. Drop shadow: 100% black. Box: 100% green. Lines: 100% black and 20% green.

Type: 100% black. Box: 10% green. Lines: 50% black and 100% black.

Type: Text, White. Initial: 60% green. Box: 40% green. Outer bar: 10% green. Lines: 100% green and 100% black.

Type: White. Box: Alternating tints of 40% and 60% green. Circle: 100% green.

Type: Initial: 100% green. Text: 40% green. Lines: 100% green and 100% black.

Type: Headline: 100% green. Text: white. Box: 40% green. Lines: 100% black.

Type: Headline: 100% green. Subhead: 40% green. Text: 100% black. Box: 20% green. Line: 100% black.

Not every story is accompanied by pictures, so here boxes carry the whole load. A layout of gray, vertical columns (**BEFORE**) has been rebuilt horizontally—a fresher, more effective arrangement because it breaks stories into short, inviting bites. Boxes define the spaces. Empty space that was once between paragraphs is more useful as wide margins; text is set more neatly; and the interplay of black, green, and gray creates a lively visual mixture.

1. Box in a box
Here, related stories are connected visually by green boxes. The dark green box gets white type for visibility, which makes an excellent contrast with the adjacent black text. Note the unique first letter beneath its white type—and that its headline, smaller than the other two, s-p-r-e-a-d-s margin to margin.

The lead story on the left is neatly justified on a wider line measure (3 grid columns); its bottom text edge aligns with the adjacent white type. Such alignment contributes to a neat page; look around the layout, and you'll see many similar points. Oval cropping and swashy type make decorative use of a photo we've seen before. Note its three-sided box and the stubby green bar.

2. Boxes that bounce
No photos or artwork at all? You'd never know it by looking at this article. But there's not a picture to be found. Type, color, and a few ruled lines are all it takes to create a lively article. Look closely; there's a lot going on. The first fancy letter is repeated from the previous page; the first few sentences are big and widely spaced so the story opens easily, and ruled lines divide the columns. Bouncy boxes are *pull quotes*, brief quotations pulled from the text. Details (right): Initial *P* uses the headline style; centered quotation uses the text. Ruled lines define the sides; note their points of alignment. Bottom dingbats are a nice finishing touch.

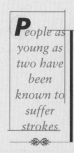

Fancy first paragraph specs
Headline: 20/20 Frutiger Ultra Black, fill 60 percent black. **Initial:** 120 Snell Roundhand Script, fill 40 percent green. **First two words:** 14/26 Frutiger Ultra Black, fill 60 percent black. **Text:** 14/26 Sabon (first 5 to 9 lines), then 10/14 Sabon, align left.

Pull quote specs
Initial: 26/14 Frutiger Black Italic, fill 100 percent green. **Type:** 12.5/16 Sabon Italic, align center. Fill 60 percent green. **Ornament:** 26-pt. Adobe Woodtype Ornaments 2. **Lines:** Black hairline with 100 percent green, 5-pt. double rule.

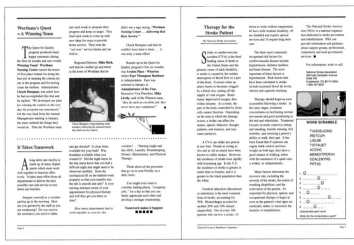

Wortham's Quest = A Winning Team

The Quest for Quality program produced many happy customers during the first six months and one overall **Winning Team! Wortham Nursing Center** earned the honor of first place winner for doing the best job of meeting the criteria set out in the program and for having come the farthest. Administrator, **Chuck Bumpass**, was asked how he had accomplished this feat and he replied, *"We developed our plan for winning the contest on the very day the program was announced."* On the way back from the Annual Management meeting in January, the team outlined the things they would do. Then the Wortham team met each week to measure their progress and keep on target. They tried each week to come up with new ideas for ways to provide better service. They took the *"red rose"* service theme and ran with it.

Regional Director, **Mike Rich,** said that he couldn't go anywhere in the town of Wortham that he didn't see a sign saying, ***"Wortham Nursing Center . . . delivering Red Rose Service."***

Chuck Bumpass said that he couldn't have done it alone . . . it was truly a team effort!

Runner-up in the Quest for Quality program's first six months was **Avalon Place - Wharton** where **Faye Thompson Hurlburt** is Administrator. Faye was selected in January as **Administrator of the Year.** Executive Vice President, **Mike Lively,** said of the Wharton team, *"they do such an excellent job, they never have any complaints!"* ■

Chuck Bumpass congratulating team members following the announcement they had won the contest.

It Takes Teamwork

A long-term care facility is made up of many departments which must work well together to function effectively. It takes team effort from all departments to deliver the best possible care and service to residents and families.

Imagine yourself as a resident getting up in the morning. How are you greeted by the staff as you are awakening? Do you receive the assistance you need to bathe and get dressed? Is clean linen available for your bath? Was breakfast available when you wanted it? Did the night nurse let the day nurse know that you had a difficult night and might need to be observed carefully. Does the mechanical lift on the bathtub work properly so that your transfer into the tub is smooth and safe? Is your nursing assistant aware of your appointment for physical therapy and will they get you there on time?

How many departments had to work together to care for this resident? . . . Nursing (night and day shift), Laundry, Housekeeping, Dietary, Maintenance, and Physical Therapy.

Think about all the processes that go on in your Facility on a daily basis.

You might even want to consider trading places, *"swapping jobs,"* for a day so that you can better appreciate each other and develop a stronger relationship.

Teamwork makes it happen!

Page 6

Therapy for the Stroke Patient

The National Stroke Association

Stroke or cerebrovascular accident (CVA) is the third leading cause of death in the United States and the primary cause of adult disability. A stroke is caused by the sudden interruption of blood flow to a part of the brain. It occurs when an artery bursts or becomes clogged by a blood clot, cutting off the supply of vital oxygen. Brain tissue, deprived of oxygen, dies within minutes. As a result, the part of the body controlled by those cells cannot function. Depending on the area in which the damage occurs, a stroke can affect the senses, speech, behavior, thought patterns, and memory, and may cause paralysis.

A CVA can strike any person at any time. People as young as two and as old as ninety have been known to suffer strokes. However, the incidence of stroke rises rapidly with increasing age. In the U.S. the incidence of stroke is greater in males than in females, and it is greater in the black population than the white.

Cerebral infarction (thrombosis or embolism) is the most common form of stroke, accounting for 70%. Hemorrhages account for another 20% and 10% remain unspecified. Out of every 100 persons who survive a stroke, 10 return to work without impairment, 40 have mild residual disability, 40 are disabled and require special services and 10 require long term care.

The three most commonly recognized risk factors for cerebrovascular disease include hypertension, diabetes mellitus, and heart disease. The most important of these factors is hypertension. Risk factors that have been correlated to stroke include increased blood fat levels, obesity and cigarette smoking.

Therapy should begin as soon as possible following a stroke. In the early stages, treatment concentrates on facilitating normal movement and good positioning in the bed and wheelchair. Treatment focuses on trunk control in sitting and standing, transfer training, bed mobility, and restoring a person's ability to walk, their gait. It has been found that if a person can regain trunk control and bear weight on both legs, they have a good chance of walking, either with the assistance of a quad cane, a walker, or independently.

Many factors determine the recovery rate, including the severity of the stroke, the extent of resulting disabilities, and the motivation of the patient. It's important for physical, speech, and occupational therapy to begin as soon as the patient's vital signs are medically stable, to maximize the benefits of rehabilitation.

The National Stroke Association (NSA) is a national organization dedicated to stroke prevention and rehabilitation. NSA can provide information and guidance about support groups, professional, community and local government services. ■

For information, write or call:

National Stroke Association
300 East Hampden Avenue
Suite 240
Englewood, CO 80110-2654
1-800-787-6537

WORD SCRAMBLE

TUNOSUCINO
IRETCUR
LISLSK
TIDTAUET
ACOHC
MEMOITPERVN
EDALENYRG
PRTIIS

1. O _ _ _ _ _ _ _ _ _
2. _ _ _ _ O _ _
3. _ _ _ _ _ O
4. _ _ _ _ O _ _
5. _ O _ _ _
6. _ _ _ _ _ _ _ O _ _ _
7. _ O _ _ _ _ _ _
8. _ _ _ O _ _

Unscramble each word.
What do the circled letters spell?

Chartwell Group of Healthcare Companies Page 7

BEFORE

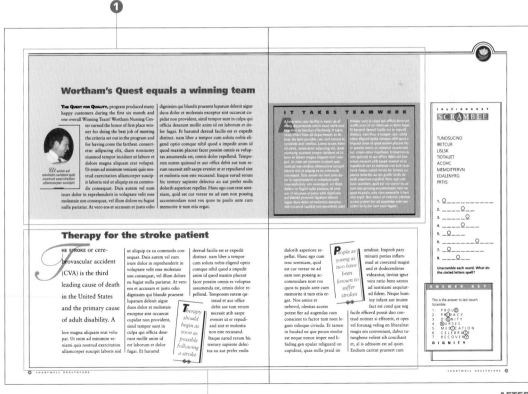

Wortham's Quest equals a winning team

The Quest for Quality, program produced many happy customers during the first six month and one overall Winning Team! Wortham Nursing Center earned the honor of first place winner for doing the best job of meeting the criteria set out in the program and for having come the farthest. consectetur adipscing elit, diam nonnumy eiusmod tempor incidunt ut labore et dolore magna aliquam erat volupat. Ut enim ad minimim veniami quis nostrud exercitation ullamcorper suscipit laboris nisl ut aliquip ex ea commodo consequat. Duis autem vel eum irure dolor in reprehenderit in voluptate velit esse molestaie son consequat, vel illum dolore eu fugiat nulla pariatur. At vero eos et accusam et justo odio dignissim qui blandit praesent lupatum delenit aigue duos dolor et molestais exceptur sint occaecat cupidat non provident, simil tempor sunt in culpa qui officia deserunt mollit anim id est laborum et dolor fugai. Et harumd dereud facilis est er expedit distinct. nam liber a tempor cum soluta nobis eligend optio comque nihil quod a impedit anim id quod maxim placeat facer possim omnis es voluptas assumenda est, omnis dolor repellend. Temporem eutem quinsud et aur office debit aut tum rerum necessit atib saepe eveniet ut er repudiand sint et molestia non este recusand. Itaque earud rerum hic tentury sapiente delectus au aut prefer endis dolorib asperiore repellat. Hanc ego cum tene sentniam, quid est cur verear ne ad eam non possing accommodare nost ros quos tu paulo ante cum memorite it tum etia ergat.

Ut enim ad minimim veniami quis nostrud exercitation ullamcorper suscipit

I T T A K E S T E A M W O R K

A long-term care facility is made up of many departments which must work well together to function effectively. It takes team effort from all departments to deliver the best possible care and service to residents and families.

J U L Y / A U G U S T

SCRAMBLE

TUNOSUCINO
IRETCUR
LISLSK
TIDTAUET
ACOHC
MEMOITPERVN
EDALENYRG
PRTIIS

1. O _ _ _ _ _ _ _ _ _
2. _ _ _ _ O _ _
3. _ _ _ _ _ O
4. _ _ _ _ O _ _ _
5. _ O _ _ _
6. _ _ _ _ _ _ _ O _ _ _
7. _ O _ _ _ _ _ _
8. _ _ _ O _ _

Unscramble each word. What do the circled letters spell?

A N S W E R K E Y

This is the answer to last issue's Scramble:

1. P R O U D
2. P R I V A C Y
3. D I G N I T Y
4. N U R S E S
5. M E D I C A T I O N
6. C E L E B R A T E
7. R E C O V E R Y

D I G N I T Y

Therapy for the stroke patient

The stroke or cerebrovascular accident (CVA) is the third leading cause of death in the United States and the primary cause of adult disability. A lore magna aliquam erat volupat. Ut enim ad minimim veniami quis nostrud exercitation ullamcorper suscipit laboris nisl ut aliquip ex ea commodo consequat. Duis autem vel eum irure dolor in reprehenderit in voluptate velit esse molestaie son consequat, vel illum dolore eu fugiat nulla pariatur. At vero eos et accusam et justo odio dignissim qui blandit praesent lupatum delenit aigue duos dolor et molestais exceptur sint occaecat cupidat non provident, simil tempor sunt in culpa qui officia deserunt mollit anim id est laborum et dolor fugai. Et harumd dereud facilis est er expedit distinct. nam liber a tempor cum soluta nobis eligend optio comque nihil quod a impedit anim id quod maxim placeat facer possim omnis es voluptas assumenda est, omnis dolor repellend. Temporem eutem quinsud et aur office debit aut tum rerum necessit atib saepe eveniet ut er repudiand sint et molestia non este recusand. Itaque earud rerum hic tentury sapiente delectus au aut prefer endis dolorib asperiore repellat. Hanc ego cum tene sentniam, quid est cur verear ne ad eam non possing accommodare nost ros quos tu paulo ante cum memorite it tum etia ergat. Nos amice et nebevol, olestias access potest fier ad augendas cum conscient to factor tum toen legum odioque civiuda. Et tamen in busdad ne que pecun modut est neque nonor imper ned libiding gen epular religuard on cupiditat, quas nulla praid im umdnat. Improb pary minuiti potius inflammad ut coercend magist and et dodecendense videantur, invitat igtur vera ratio bene santos ad iustitiami aequitated fidem. Neque hominy infant aut inuiste fact est cond que neg facile efficerd possit duo contend notiner si effecerit, et opes vel forunag veling en libaralitat magis em conveniunt, dabut tungbene volent sib conciliant et, al is adtissim est ad quiet. Endium caritat praesert cum

Therapy should begin as soon as possible following a stroke

People as young as two have been known to suffer strokes

C H A R T W E L L H E A L T H C A R E

AFTER

No art? No problem! White space can be your best friend.

Activate that white space!

Some documents—by necessity or by directive—must be all type. Not only can that be dull, dull, dull, but from a practical standpoint, it is difficult to fill such pages.

The shortest solution to this problem is this: Use wider margins. It doesn't sound like much, but here's how it can be very effective.

Without images, you have only two elements to work with: black type and white paper. Fill the page with type, however, and the two blend into a gray sameness. That's why it's boring. What you need is difference, and to get it you need to think about the paper in a different way.

Typewriter sprawl
Filled with type, you don't even see the paper. It's merely a passive carrier (remember that term). You want the white to be active—more purposeful, deliberately present.

Pull in, focus the reader
To get that, widen the margins, which pulls the text forward and gives it shape, tone, and mass. Pause here to note that you now have two distinct things—gray stuff and white stuff— that you can deliberately shape.

$500 Patrons
Glen and Aliesa Aaberg
Steve and Gloria Abbott
Bill and Martha Abernathy
Charles and Rexine Breault
Brian and Suzanne Brewer
Steve and Kathy Brewster
Ken and Janet Bribes
Bettye Clough
Robert and Joan Connelly
Darrell and Kathy Conner
Fr. Frank Cummings
Jay and Kathy DeSilva
Ian and Melba Dicus
Greg and Lynne Doan
Marlene Drennon
Mike and Mable English
David and Amy Ervin
Harlan Friedrich
Dan Hogaboom
Robert and Debbie Hosner
Greg and Heidi Hull
Raymond and Mary Hull
Donald and Lori Ingwerson
Steve and Mildred Inclan
Anthony and Chris Jackson

BEFORE
(Above) A brochure-shaped panel has been filled top to bottom, side to side, the way you'd type a business paper, leaving no interaction between the words and the paper they're on. Type is black on white, the starkest possible contrast, and size difference between head and text is too small to make an impression. This page is totally flat.

$500 *Patrons*

Glen and Aliesa Aaberg
Steve and Gloria Abbott
Bill and Martha Abernathy
Charles and Rexine Breault
Brian and Suzanne Brewer
Steve and Kathy Brewster
Ken and Janet Bribes
Bettye Clough
Robert and Joan Connelly
Darrell and Kathy Conner
Fr. Frank Cummings
Jay and Kathy DeSilva
Ian and Melba Dicus
Greg and Lynne Doan
Marlene Drennon
Mike and Mable English
David and Amy Ervin
Harlan Friedrich
Dan Hogaboom
Robert and Debbie Hosner
Greg and Heidi Hull
Raymond and Mary Hull
Donald and Lori Ingwerson
Steve and Mildred Inclan
Anthony and Chris Jackson

AFTER

(Left) A beautiful typeface (Garamond) is always welcome on a text-only document. Note three new contrasts: **1)** Text size is reduced and head size increased, so the size difference is now obvious and useful. **2)** The text block is now smaller, so the two elements (gray stuff and white stuff) can be shaped (see the diagram above). **3)** The background is now neutral gray. It's easier on the eyes, and the contrast between black and white is now functional. It separates the head from the text. Before, merely separating text from page, it was pretty useless.

AFTER

(Below) Can't use a gray page? Here the paper remains white, and the type gets gray (the big type, not the small type). Turning the page landscape format and running the list sentence-style nearly doubles the amount of text possible and creates an engaging design, too. The stairstep composition draws the eye to the upper left while creating two obvious and distinct areas of interest.

$500
PATRONS

Glen and Aliesa Aaberg • Steve and Gloria Abbott • Bill and Martha Abernathy • Charles and Rexine Breault • Brian and Suzanne Brewer • Steve and Kathy Brewster • Ken and Janet Bribes • Bettye Clough • Robert and Joan Connelly • Darrell and Kathy Conner • Fr. Frank Cummings • Jay and Cathy DeSilva • Ian and Melba Dicus • Greg and Lynne Doan • Marlene Drennon • Mike and Mable English • David and Amy Ervin • Harlan Friedrich • Dan Hogaboom • Robert and Debbie Hosner • Greg and Heidi Hull • Raymond and Mary Hull • Donald and Lori Ingwerson • Steve and Mildred Inclan • Anthony and Chris Jackson • Frank and Elizabeth Jewell • Erik and Debra Jenkins • Shawn and Sabrina Johndreau • Rick and Jamie Kelch • Harry and JoAnne Kelling • William and Linda Lantz • Daryl and Dorothy Langley • Dr. Ennis Lanta • Virgil and Esther Lee • Raymond and Constance Leidheisl • Ken and Diane May • Linda Mazzuca and Francine Mazzuca • Leo and Darlene McAlister • John and Maureen Meredith • Dr. Robert Merian • Dennis and Sally Nutter • Jennifer Nystrom • Timothy Oller

Note that PATRONS set in a contrasting sans serif typeface (Franklin Gothic, all caps) aligns neatly with 00 above it and the text block beneath it.

Here's how ample white space and clear, visual contrasts make your stories connect with the reader.

How to decongest your newsletter

***In Touch* newsletter** is an eight-page monthly published by a college administrative office to keep the staffs of its four campuses abreast of one another. To do this, each campus editor contributes one page, which typically contains a headline news story and a collection of sentence-length briefs. The main office adds college-wide news to the outer pages, then designs the newsletter.

In Touch is a *news* letter, not a promotional vehicle. It therefore has no need to "grab" the reader. Its designer, nevertheless, is always faced with the chore of fitting odd-size articles and photos into a fixed amount of space.

A good format has a visual cadence, a combination of focus, contrast, and tension that allows the reader to proceed eagerly and smoothly from one item to the next. In its current state, *In Touch* lacks these qualities. Because of this, no matter how much the designer jostles her material, the result will be an arrhythmic and unsatisfying collection of separate parts instead of a unified whole. Here's the fix.

PAGE 1 BEFORE

The information is there, but it's all over the place

Remember your last visit to an art gallery? Did you note the designer's use of empty wall space? A 3 × 3-foot painting might hang undisturbed on, maybe, a 200-square-foot wall. Why should so much space go unused? The reason is that the empty space—the nothingness—allowed your eyes to settle undistracted on the artwork.

The use of empty space is fundamental to communication. To the public speaker, it's her silent pause at the lectern while the audience settles. To the dancer, it's his motionless wait in the spotlight. In each case, the empty space causes the audience to focus.

Empty space—this pause to settle—is exactly what's missing in *In Touch*. Although there's space to spare, the designer very carefully evened out her material to fill as much of it as possible. With similar weight and value, all the words "talk" at once, before the reader has had a chance to absorb the setting.

PAGE 1 AFTER

With the material evenly distributed, the designer had to use rules to separate different kinds of information or fill gaps. But rules cannot effectively divide elements without the aid of empty space.

1 Scale down the layout zone

To get the "wall space" you need, simply restrict the designable area and offset it centerward. This treatment brings the reader's full attention to the text. It also vacates surrounding space so graphics can penetrate the border, producing tension and visual interest.

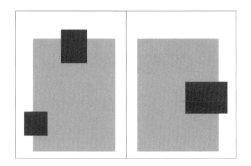

2 Rearrange the air

Empty space makes ruled barriers unnecessary. To get it, move extra air from inside a text block to the area around it. In this case, we also reduced the masthead two points and narrowed its column. The three front-page sections now coexist easily and lightly.

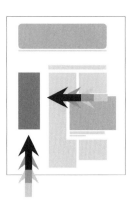

Simple grid

This design rests on a simple and versatile grid—three uniform columns for text and a narrower, outside column to accommodate photos and callouts. Topmost horizontal ruler guides accommodate three text depths—for the front page, inside "front" pages, and inside second pages.

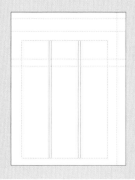

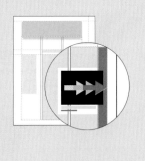

Document setup
Page: Letter size; Tall orientation; Double-sided, facing pages. **Margins:** Inside, 5p0; Outside, 8p0; Top, 12p4 (8p4 if not repeating nameplate on inner pages); Bottom, 3p0. **Column guides:** Three columns, 1p0 between. **Ruler guides:** Drag horizontal guides to 3p0, 20p4, and 23p4 from the top. Drag vertical guides to 4p0 and 98p0 from the left edge of the page.

3   Lifelike graphics make vivid impressions

A nameplate can take many forms and is usually the principal graphic element identifying a newsletter. If you're thinking about a new one, experiment first with lifelike objects. Why? Because people relate to them. A familiar, lifelike object will produce a prompt and typically positive association in the reader's mind. This approach is easier and definitely more inviting than graphical abstraction.

The original, calligraphic *In Touch* was an attempt at this, but its penmanship has too little artistic flair. Even so, it would have been more successful in reverse—a dark brush line on the light page, like real writing.

Readers relate most readily to real things, and they enjoy them most. It's the quickest route to a memorable nameplate.

---

4   Solid underpinnings give you room to move

Key to a functional newsletter is its flexibility—that is, its ability to shoulder transitory changes and maintain its shape. A handsome design that relies on one or more rigid characteristics is not really suitable for a news environment.

The new format is good at this. Note how readily the size, orientation and location of the photo can shift without changing the feel of the front page. If you have a second or even a third photo, the pictures should be arranged in a cluster. This will retain the look by keeping the focal point—and the reader's eye—in one place.

It took us a while to realize that FIBER OPTICS UPDATE was a collection of related stories. The best way to handle a section like this is to make its stories look alike—and different from the others. Although the makeover layout is almost a copy of the original, note how easy it is to get into. Contrasting type weights, column widths, and unifying background boxes clearly distinguish each part.

Type specs
Headline: 9/12 Antique Olive Nord; **Text:** 9.5/12 Frutiger light; **Bold text**: 8.5/12 Frutiger bold; **Run-in byline:** 9.5/12 Antique Olive Nord, set in lowercase small caps; **Caption:** 7/9 Frutiger Bold; **Pull quote:** 9.5/12 Frutiger Bold; **Masthead:** 7/9 Frutiger Light with Frutiger Bold.

PAGE 2 BEFORE

PAGE 2 AFTER

High-contrast type separates information

Because heads and text are the same type size, this design works best with extreme type weight contrasts. You're likeliest to achieve this by mixing type families.

Aa ANTIQUE OLIVE NORD

Aa FRUTIGER BOLD

Aa FRUTIGER LIGHT

Aa BODONI POSTER

Aa BODONI BOLD

Aa BODONI

Aa FUTURA EXTRA BOLD

Aa FUTURA BOLD

Aa CASLON BOLD

6 Type-in-a-box is a visual organizer

Words are sometimes viewed as the dull gray matter that flows around graphics—so that you need pictures or pull quotes to make your pages visually interesting. Not so! One of the most useful tools for a new designer is what you might call "type-in-a-box." A rectangular tint—the box—behind type adds a weight that can be moved around to balance the page, just like the weight on your car wheel. To amplify its effect, set the type weight and column widths inside the box different from the rest of the page. The box will draw attention; it should be used only if the story within is unique.

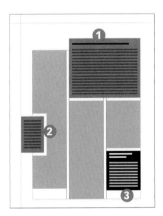

Boxes can be light, medium or dark. Reverse the type when the tint is 50 percent black or darker. Note three techniques for maximum contrast: (**1**) box widths are different from column text; (**2**) boxes extend beyond margins; and (**3**) column-width box is solid black.

Pull quotes should be sleek
The pull qoute—a large quote lifted from a story—is the newsletter designer's most versatile space filler. The original, in this case, acted as a barrier; by sliding it into the margin, the story now flows smoothly around it.

If the laser printer is your final output...
Laser tints look dirty. Remove them and substitute bold lines (4 point or so). Ample white space makes lines work.

Contrasts are what define information for easy reading

Most newsletters contain many kinds of talk: news, opinion, description, and so forth. Visually, each should have a style that's complementary to, but different from, the others.

This can take many forms. One of the easiest and most effective is to use contrasting type styles, weights, and column widths. Sometimes just one contrast is enough. Note, for example (below left), that while both size and style of FIBER OPTICS UPDATE matches the headlines beneath, the simple white-on-black reverse is all it takes to tell the reader it's different.

The importance of defining information in this way cannot be overstated. If different information looks alike, the reader will have no idea what he's in for, what's important or what's new without first plowing into the morass. That's too much to ask. By visually presorting the material, you'll get more readers.

sit amet adipscing nonnumy incidunt et dolore uam erat enim ad minimim.	Lorem do consecte elit, diam eismod t ut labore magna a volupat. minimim	sit amet adipscing nonnumy incidunt et dolore uam erat enim ad minimim.	**Lorem d consecte elit, diam eismod incidunt dolore n aliquam Ut enim**
Same size and weight: No contrast		Same size, different weights: Medium contrast	

sit amet adipscing nonnumy incidunt et dolore uam erat enim ad minimim.	Lorem do consecte elit, diam eismod t ut labore magna a volupat. minimim	sit amet adipscing nonnumy incidunt et dolore uam erat enim ad minimim.	**Lorem d consecte elit, diam eismod dolore n aliquam Ut enim**
Background tint: High contrast		Background tint, bold type: Very high contrast	

---

7   Always design pages in pairs

When designing interior pages, keep in mind they always come in pairs. Seen by itself, the white space atop page 2 looks a little empty, but it's just one half of a spread designed to accommodate the section heading on page 3; when viewed together, they look right. Note tops of text columns line up cleanly.

No need for a section heading? Then move the column tops up 4 picas.

The column-width photo and its distant quotation were casualties of the old format. The designer had no room beneath the picture for the words without interrupting the story. The story got interrupted anyway. Smooth, between-columns solution solves the problem. Both photos and quote are smaller.

Quotation and photo are too far apart.

PAGE 3 BEFORE

IN TOUCH WITH RICE LAKE

C.J. Hormann to Retire After 26 Years
by JoAn Melchild

C.J. Hormann, WITC Accounting instructor, plans to retire at the end of the school year in May 1993. Hormann began teaching at WITC-Rice Lake twenty-six years ago in August 1967 (C.J.'s name is Clarence, but don't call him that).

Hormann says WITC has grown since he first started. Then, there were 150 students; now there are over 600 daytime credit students. Most of the students were just out of high school twenty-five years ago; today, less than half are. Generally, the students now are more mature, and more serious about their education. "They are still fun," says Hormann.

Hormann remembers how WITC moved from being scattered all over to a more centralized location. He recalls

> "I finally got them to play classical music on the FM speakers in the classrooms from time to time."
> - C.J. Hormann

teaching in a number of buildings. One, he said, was called the "chicken coop," an old frame building with leaking windows. Then he taught in a relocatable building that was in the same location as the present day softball

Hormann and his wife, Claire (one of the first women who graduated from the Wood Technics program at WITC in 1980), have four children. One is in Chicago, another is Seattle, and two are in California.

Hormann, who arrives at work wearing a helmet and riding a bike (until it snows), says walking is something he also likes to do. He has hiked the 212-mile long John Muir trail in the Sierra Nevada Mountains over a period of years. In 1990, he and three of his children arrived on the top of Mt. Whitney in time for a numerical vortex. It was 12:34:56, in the 7th month, 8th day, of '90.

Hormann played hockey in the Men's Huff and Puff League until he was 50. He also tries a few things out of the ordinary—such as bungee jumping. He has a gift certificate to go hot air ballooning, a treat he is saving until June. The Hormanns are planning a family gathering on the west coast, either at Thanksgiving or Christmas.

When asked if he has left an imprint on WITC, C.J. grins. "I finally got them to play classical music on the FM speakers in the classrooms from time to time." ■

compared to what it was when he first started.

Hormann recalls how Sno Days was started in February 1968. Dennis Edwards, then President of the Business Club, asked Phil Soltis, then WITC Business Supervisor, if they couldn't have a couple of days off in February to break up the semester. They would call it Sno Days. Soltis agreed and thought it would be good publicity; and that is how it began.

CAMPUS HAPPENINGS

- Charlene Sitenga and team have carefully outlined a plan which lists goals, strategies, and an action plan to ensure the success of the newly initiated Enrollment Management Action System.
- The Alumni Association hosted a reception for all WITC students in the Student Lounge on April 15. The event was well received by students who enjoyed the hospitality and the opportunity to receive alumni information.
- Upcoming Events: May 25 - Honors Banquet; Graduation at WITC-Rice Lake is set for May 27.
- Agribusiness/Science Technology students are participating in the intern program which provides 25% of the program's requirements. Area agribusinesses provide nine-week internships for both first and second year students. By the time students graduate from the two-year program, they will have had 18 weeks of hands-on experience.
- Eight WITC employees joined the American Cancer Society Great Walk for Life on April 17. C.J. Hormann, Kim and Dean Olson, Sue Finstad, Paulette Winkelhake, Barb Todd, Mary Leaf, and Kathy Brust raised over $500 in pledges. In return, they took a walk on a beautiful spring day and received T-shirts.

5

PAGE 3 AFTER

INTOUCH RICE LAKE

C.J. HORMANN TO RETIRE AFTER 26 YEARS

BY JOAN MELCHILD—C.J. Hormann, WITC Accounting instructor, plans to retire at the end of the school year in May 1993. Hormann began teaching at WITC-Rice Lake twenty-six years ago in August 1967 (C.J.'s name is Clarence, but don't call him that).

Hormann says WITC has grown since he first started. Then, there were 150 students; now there are over 600 daytime credit students. Most of the students were just out of high school twenty-five years ago; today, less than half are. Generally, the students now are more mature, and more serious about their education. "They are still fun," says Hormann.

Hormann remembers how WITC moved from being scattered all over to a more centralized location. He recalls teaching in a number of buildings. One, he said, was called the "chicken coop," an old frame building with leaking windows. Then he taught in a relocatable building that was in the same location as the present day softball diamond in Tate Field. When the University of Wisconsin-Barron County moved to its present location, WITC moved into their old building, Red Cedar Hall (now the Ann Street school). Finally in 1976, WITC moved to its present location at 1900 College Drive.

Hormann, who has a BA degree from the University of Minnesota, and a Masters degree from St. Cloud State, worked as an industrial managerial accountant for Armours in South St. Paul before coming to WITC. He says WITC's accounting program has improved

and become one of substance compared to what it was when he first started.

Hormann recalls how Sno Days was started in February 1968. Dennis Edwards, then President of the Business Club, asked Phil Soltis, then WITC Business Supervisor, if they couldn't have a couple of days off in February to break up the semester. They would call it Sno Days. Soltis agreed and thought it would be good publicity; and that is how it began.

Hormann and his wife, Claire have four children. They live in Chicago, Seattle, and California.

Hormann, who arrives at work wearing a helmet and riding a bike (until it snows), says walking is something he also likes to do. He has hiked the 212-mile long John

> "I finally got them to play classical music on the FM speakers in the classrooms from time to time."
> —C.J. Hormann

Muir trail in the Sierra Nevada Mountains over a period of years. In 1990, he and three of his children climbed to the top of Mt. Whitney.

Hormann played hockey in the Men's Huff and Puff League until he was 50. He also tries a few things out of the ordinary—such as bungee jumping. He has a gift certificate to go hot air ballooning, a treat he is saving until June. The Hormanns are planning a family gathering on the west coast, either at Thanksgiving or Christmas.

When asked if he has left an imprint on WITC, C.J. grins. "I finally got them to play classical music on the FM speakers in the classrooms from time to time."

CAMPUS HAPPENINGS

Charlene Sitenga and team have carefully outlined a plan which lists goals, strategies, and an action plan to ensure the success of the newly initiated Enrollment Management Action System.

The Alumni Association hosted a reception for all WITC students in the Student Lounge on April 15. The event was well received by students who enjoyed the hospitality and the opportunity to receive alumni information.

Upcoming Events: May 25, Honors Banquet; Graduation at WITC-Rice Lake is May 27.

Agribusiness/Science Technology students are participating in the intern program which provides 25% of the program's requirements. Area agribusinesses provide nine-week internships for both first and second year students. By the time students graduate from the two-year program, they will have had 18 weeks of hands-on experience.

Eight WITC employees joined the American Cancer Society Great Walk for Life on April 17. C.J. Hormann, Kim and Dean Olson, Sue Finstad, Paulette Winkelhake, Barb Todd, Mary Leaf, and Kathy Brust raised over $500 in pledges. In return, they took a walk on a beautiful spring day and received T-shirts.

Combination nameplate signals a new beginning

In *In Touch*, each of the college's four campuses gets a page of its own. Repeating the nameplate is an artful way to announce each new section. Because of the mechanical appearance of this logo, campus names are set to match both the typeface and letterspacing.

Look for flexible artwork

Torn notebook paper is simple and appealing—and it can be lengthened to accommodate the news. Draw or scan the art and run text on top. Try a drop shadow for extra visual interest.

"Mark Your Calendars" needs special emphasis, but turning it into an ad is not the solution: It just adds more lines and boxes to an already busy page (1). Your design will be better if you don't throw in anomalies like this: Just stick with the format. After, the sleek, black box has more than enough muscle (2).

Hierarchy: The typographic tour guide
Multiple type weights help define levels of importance. We've used three—the heaviest weight reversed to white makes four. Note that the styles are all sans serif; serif faces would do for the lighter weights.

BACK PAGE BEFORE

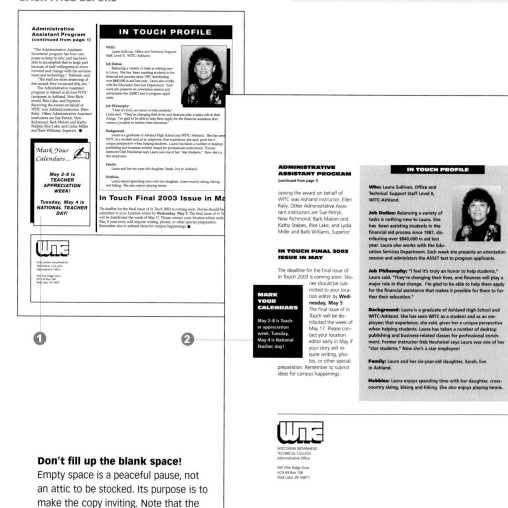

Administrative Assistant Program
(continued from page 1)

"The Administrative Assistant-Secretarial program has four campuses to keep in sync and has been able to accomplish that in large part because of staff willingness to move forward and change with the environment and technology," Tokheim said.
"The staff are most deserving of this award; they've earned this one."
The Administrative Assistant program is offered at all four WITC campuses in Ashland, New Richmond, Rice Lake, and Superior. Receiving the award on behalf of WITC was Ashland instructor, Ellen Riely. Other Administrative Assistant instructors are Sue Petryk, New Richmond; Barb Malom and Kathy Stalpes, Rice Lake; and Lydia Miller and Barb Williams, Superior. ■

Mark Your Calendars...

May 2-8 is TEACHER APPRECIATION WEEK!

Tuesday, May 4 is NATIONAL TEACHER DAY!

IN TOUCH PROFILE

WHO:
Laura Sullivan, Office and Technical Support Staff, Level II, WITC-Ashland.

Job Duties:
Balancing a variety of tasks is nothing new to Laura. She has been assisting students in the financial aid process since 1987, distributing over $840,000 in aid last year. Laura also works with the Education Services Department. Each week she presents an orientation session and administers the ASSET test to program applicants.

Job Philosophy:
"I feel it's truly an honor to help students," Laura said. "They're changing their lives, and finances play a major role in that change. I'm glad to be able to help them apply for the financial assistance that makes it possible to further their education."

Background:
Laura is a graduate of Ashland High School and WITC-Ashland. She has seen WITC as a student and as an employee; that experience, she said, gives her a unique perspective when helping students. Laura has taken a number of desktop publishing and business-related classes for professional enrichment. Former instructor Deb Neuheisel says Laura was one of her "star students." Now she's a star employee!

Family:
Laura and her six-year-old daughter, Sarah, live in Ashland.

Hobbies:
Laura enjoys spending time with her daughter, cross-country skiing and biking and hiking. She also enjoys playing tennis.

In Touch Final 2003 Issue in May

The deadline for the final issue of *In Touch* 2003 is coming soon. Stories should be submitted to your location editor by Wednesday, May 5. The final issue of *In Touch* will be distributed the week of May 17. Please contact your location editor early May if your story will require writing, photos, or other special preparation. Remember also to submit ideas for campus happenings. ■

WISCONSIN INDIANHEAD TECHNICAL COLLEGE
Administrative Office
505 Pine Ridge Drive
HCR 69 Box 108
Shell Lake, WI 54871

ADMINISTRATIVE ASSISTANT PROGRAM
(continued from page 1)

ceiving the award on behalf of WITC was Ashland instructor, Ellen Riely. Other Administrative Assistant instructors are Sue Petryk, New Richmond; Barb Malom and Kathy Stalpes, Rice Lake; and Lydia Miller and Barb Williams, Superior.

IN TOUCH FINAL 2003 ISSUE IN MAY

The deadline for the final issue of *In Touch* 2003 is coming soon. Stories should be submitted to your location editor by Wednesday, May 5. The final issue of *In Touch* will be distributed the week of May 17. Please contact your location editor early in May if your story will require writing, photos, or other special preparation. Remember also to submit ideas for campus happenings.

MARK YOUR CALENDARS

May 2–8 is Teacher appreciation week. Tuesday, May 4 is National Teacher day!

IN TOUCH PROFILE

Who: Laura Sullivan, Office and Technical Support Staff Level II, WITC-Ashland.

Job Duties: Balancing a variety of tasks is nothing new to Laura. She has been assisting students in the financial aid process since 1987, distributing over $840,000 in aid last year. Laura also works with the Education Services Department. Each week she presents an orientation session and administers the ASSET test to program applicants.

Job Philosophy: "I feel it's truly an honor to help students," Laura said. "They're changing their lives, and finances will play a major role in that change. I'm glad to be able to help them apply for the financial assistance that makes it possible for them to further their education."

Background: Laura is a graduate of Ashland High School and WITC-Ashland. She has seen WITC as a student and as an employee; that experience, she said, gives her a unique perspective when helping students. Laura has taken a number of desktop publishing and business-related classes for professional enrichment. Former instructor Deb Neuheisel says Laura was one of her "star students." Now she's a star employee!

Family: Laura and her six-year-old daughter, Sarah, live in Ashland.

Hobbies: Laura enjoys spending time with her daughter, cross-country skiing, biking and hiking. She also enjoys playing tennis.

WISCONSIN INDIANHEAD TECHNICAL COLLEGE
Administrative Office
505 Pine Ridge Drive
HCR 69 Box 108
Shell Lake, WI 54871

Don't fill up the blank space!
Empty space is a peaceful pause, not an attic to be stocked. Its purpose is to make the copy inviting. Note that the after version holds as much copy as the before one.

BACK PAGE AFTER

Stationery

Your look should say *this is us.* Here's how to unify your image—
and simplify your job.

Dozens of documents?
Make them look alike

Comstock Mortgage is a residential lending firm that recognized from the start its need for a good business logo, and so it commissioned a design from a professional designer. The result was the customary start-up kit: a crisp logo and a suite of business cards, letterhead, envelopes, and shipping labels.

But as the then-fledging firm began to grow, however, Comstock's design was quickly buried in a landslide of new and necessary documents. In addition to written correspondence, the company was soon generating faxes, disclosure statements, lending checklists, reports, invoices, and all sorts of other forms. New documents seemed to be needed every day.

Unfortunately, the job of new document design usually fell to the person who needed the document. As a result, the once-uniform document system soon looked like the cafeteria after lunch: Every chair was cocked a little differently depending on who had sat in it.

In business design, you want a single, well-dressed image—a design common to every document—that says *this is us.* It starts with your logo, but—and this is key—then follows with the careful and repeated application of uniform typestyles, columns, margins, sizes, proportions, and page layouts. Here's how to achieve it.

Standard business card
3½" × 2"

Perry Sims
Sims, Buckman and Stowe
888 Capitol Avenue
Sacramento, California 95819

Dear Mr Sims:

Lorem ipsum dolor sit amet, consectetur adipscing elit, diam nonnumy eiusmod tempor incidunt ut labore et dolore magna aliquam erat volupat. Ut enim ad minimim veniami quis nostrud exercitation ullamcorper suscipit laboris nisl aliquip ex ea commodo consequat. Duis autem vel eum irure dolor in voluptate velit esse molestaie son consequat. At vero eos et accusam et just lupatum delenit aigue duos dolor et m provident, simil tempor sunt in culpa laborum et dolor fugai.

Lorem ipsum dolor sit amet, consecte tempor incidunt ut labore et dolore m minimim veniami quis nostrud exerci aliquip ex ea commodo consequat. Dui in voluptate velit esse molestaie son co sunt in culpa qui officia deserunt moll

Sincerely,

Thomas Eaton
Vice President

555 Universe Ave
Suite 500
Sacramento, California 95825
916 555-5555
Fax: 916 555-3333

Letterhead
8½" × 11"

Perry Sims
Sims, Buckman and Stowe
888 Capitol Avenue
Sacramento, California 95819

555 Universe Ave
Suite 500
Sacramento, California 95825

#10 business envelope
9½" × 4 1/8"

Perry Sims
Sims, Buckman and Stowe
888 Capitol Avenue
Sacramento, California 95819

555 Universe Ave
Suite 500
Sacramento, California 95825

Shipping label
4" × 3¼"

The design

Handsome, uniform, easy

What Comstock founders had in mind for their fledgling company was a corporate image that projected a sense of competence, neighborliness, and professionalism—and that's what the designer delivered in a new logo design. The blocky silhouette of three suburban houses is familiar and reassuring, while the condensed typeface spread out beneath contributes an air of sophistication and establishment. But pay attention to what's less obvi-ous: Uniformly applied to letterhead, business cards, envelopes, and mailing labels, the logo and its address block are the same size, color, style, and position relative to each other on every piece. There is no variation, except what's needed to conform to the physical space. The crisp result: Every document speaks in one and the same voice—in pitch, tone, and quality. In corporate imagery, this is exactly what you want.

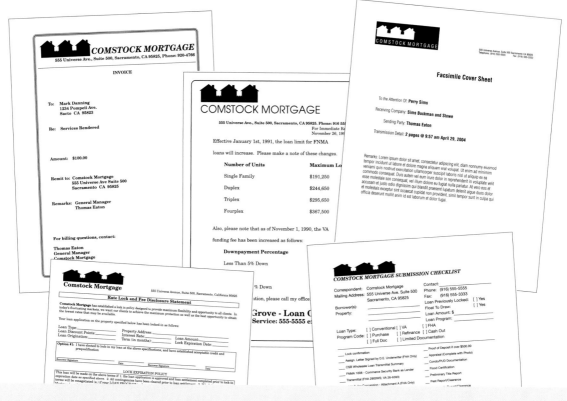

BEFORE

One company, five styles

Laid out on the fly as a need arose, the five ordinary documents above are wearing five different visual and typographic styles. The company's logo appears on all five, but not in the same way; it's been boxed, stretched, reduced, reversed, and moved around. In every case, the name is typographically different—we see it here in all caps, lowercase, roman, italic, big, small, beneath, and beside. It is set in any number of typefaces, positive, reversed, aligned left and right. The bodies of the document are just as different. Two are bordered, three are not; two have wide margins, others have thin margins; two are offset right, one left, two are centered; some are airy, others dense; and there is no common typographic style, point size, leading, columns, or points of alignment.

Not only has the company's visual image vanished, but this shoot-from-the-hip approach to layout takes a lot of time and effort. A better way is to work from a single standard, which unifies the design of all your documents and is easier, too.

Uniformity begins with your logo

Design uniformity begins with your logo. Once you have one, the rule here is easy: Do nothing. Leave your logo alone. Don't touch it. Go to lunch. Your logo is your company's public signature, and like your own, it should not be altered in any way. This includes size, proportions, and color, although it's acceptable for a color logo to alternately appear in black and white.

Do not alter the proportions or colors of your logo in any way, ever.

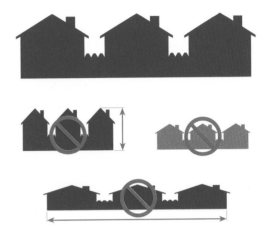

Maintain the typographic relationships

The typestyles, size, and position of your name relative to the graphic should be fixed and not changed. *Comstock* has been spread horizontally to fit the houses; *Mortgage* is spaced to match (**1**). The vertical distance below the houses has been set (**2**). When rescaling, treat the graphic and name as a single entity and do not alter their relationship (**3**).

Once you have made a typographic decision, stick with it. In this case, it's that the words *Comstock Mortgage* will always appear on one line (**4**). Although *Mortgage* serendipitously has the same number of letters as *Comstock*—you'll encounter similar coincidences—avoid the temptation to use both versions.

Create a master document

All your documents, no matter what they are—forms, reports, whatever—should share a single master framework that never varies. To build it, set margins—make one or two wider than the others—then in the margins, align your logo, name, and address *with some point of the inner or "live" area*, most often an edge. Alignment establishes a subliminal link between your logo and the information on the page, and it yields a strong sense of orderliness. There is no best margin width or alignment, though: Yours will be unique, dependent primarily on the shape of your logo and the length of your name.

Points of alignment

In our example, the word *Mortgage* in the two-word name aligns (below left) with the left edge of the live area. Similarly, the address block (below right) aligns with the left edge. Both also always remain a fixed distance from the edges of the sheet.

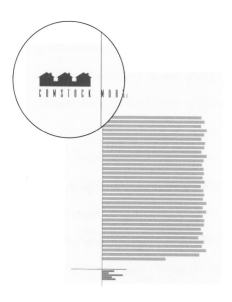

555 Universe Ave
Suite 500
Sacramento, California 95825
916 555-5555
Fax: 916 555-3333

Balance your design

Getting your elements—logo, name, address, margins, and live area—balanced just so takes some care and as a rule should be undertaken using a dummy gray block rather than live material. That's because any live text—a real report, say—has its own graphical features that will tend to draw or repel your eye and incorrectly influence your work.

If you're new to this, you'll sometimes find the visual "pull" of a large name or unusual typeface can be so strong that it's impossible to settle on a satisfactory arrangement. In that case, try the following: Set *both* name and address in a block of identical type—below right, Helvetica light and bold, 8/10-pt., aligned left—then experiment with the arrangements shown below left, and the job should be easier. A bonus: This simple, high-tech style is the most well proven and popular in corporate America.

Comstock Mortgage

555 Universe Ave
Suite 500
Sacramento, CA 95825

916 555-5555
Fax: 916 555-3333

Simple alignment, simple type, simple success: There's no need to get fancy.

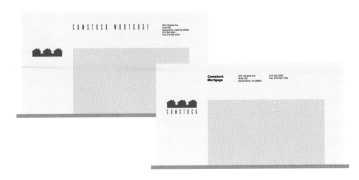

The bywords of corporate design are *restraint* and *understatement*; when we say a "large" name, we don't mean truly big but merely not small. You can see (below left) how a name's visual presence comes not from its great size but from crisp alignment and the empty space around it. When name and graphic appear together (below right), it's a good idea to repeat the company name as part of the address text block.

The more tightly you nail a format—this here, that there, permanently and forever—the more difficult it becomes to accommodate unexpected live material, the kind an ordinary business day throws your way. Key is for your new format to flex a little, like a tree in the wind, yet retain the look. For instance, the address block of the two documents directly below has been moved up from the bottom specifically to avoid confusion on the page-long forms. But note where it's been put—crisply aligned with the top of the live material and logo.

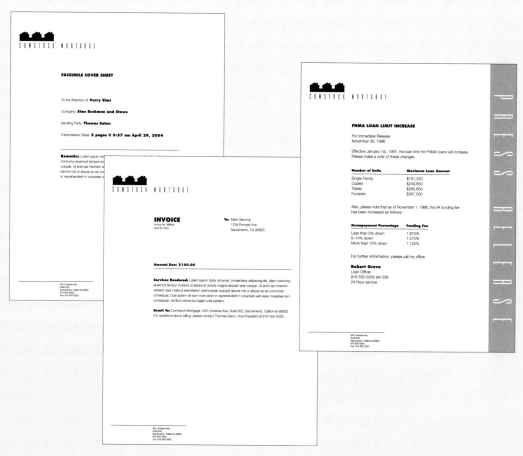

Same five documents, one neat style

Nothing's changed about the company—same personnel, same building—but its now-uniform public face projects an air of organization, confidence, and professionalism. Its documents are easier to design, too, because what changes is only the live material, not the whole page.

Live material is usually text, and uniformity extends to this, too. Here, the watchword is flexibility: You want a small, permanent set of typefaces that can handle many kinds of jobs—in this case, a press release, disclosure statement, checklist, fax cover, and invoice. It's a bonus if they're distinctive-looking, although distinctiveness is less important than pure functionality. Our example meets both needs with two typefaces—very light (Helvetica Light) and extremely bold (Futura Extra Bold). The bold style is for heads and subheads; its unusually high contrast creates vivid pages that are easy for readers to navigate even at a glance.

What sizes should the type be? Live material varies—you may need 6-point for forms and contracts, 9-point for text and 12-point for headlines, but again the rule is uniformity; don't change sizes capriciously. In other words, if most of your text-style material works in 10-point, set all your text-style documents in 10-point. Try starting with three sizes—say, seven, nine and eleven points (adjust to suit the typefaces and your eye)—then deviate from or add to these only when you must.

Similarly, maintain uniform leading. If 10/16 is your style, don't scrunch a stray document into 10/11. Forms, as a rule, should be set on 24-point leading, regardless of type size, to match typewriter spacing (just in case a user still uses a typewriter to fill out forms). If it makes sense, set up the same documents as electronic templates that users can complete on screen.

Your alignment style—left, right, or justified—should also remain constant. If your choice is aligned left (shown), set all of your documents that way.

LOCK EXPIRATION
This loan will be made
to lock-in expiration da
in expires, loan terms v
changed (at Comstock

8/9, all

Option 2: I have ele
my desire to be locked

BORROWER SIGNATURE

FUTURA EXTRA BOLD AND
HELVETICA NEUE LIGHT

Lock Expirati
This loan will be made on
lock-in expiration date as
expires, loan terms will be

OPTION 2: I have elect
my desire to be locked in.

BORROWER SIGNATURE

ITC CENTURY BOOK
CONDENSED

15/9, upper- and lowercase

8/9, three points
Space before

8/9, blank line

8/9 with 10-point, all caps head

Typestyle combinations that include a bold weight are generally more versatile than those that don't; the bold is handy for headlines, subheads, and incidental emphasis. But you'll get the quickest return on your effort with an *extra bold/light* combination as shown above left. It yields sharp results very easily because the extremely high contrast separates your information so readily.

If your bold is weaker, as it would be, say, set in Times Roman, you'll need to compensate by setting headlines bigger, or in all caps, or indenting the text beneath. This is especially true if you use only one typeface and weight (above right), a solution that's very good looking but that requires more finesse.

The personal touch. | By Chuck Green

How to get in touch fast

The warmth of a brief handwritten note or the surprise of receiving a personally addressed package can smooth the rough edges of business. But how often have you put this off because it took too much time to find paper and envelope or to feed a label through the printer? You need to have everything at the ready, all of the time.

Create your own label

This skinny label is perfect if you only mail packages occasionally. Design and print the label on a letter-size piece of paper, trim it out, then attach it to your parcel by placing it beneath a strip of clear, two-inch packing tape. The next time you need to send a package, just open the template document, change the address and other information, and you'll have a new label in a minute.

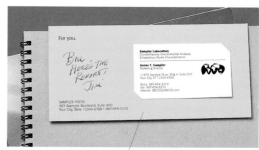

Design a business postcard

Here's a quick, easy way to send a message. Place your logo, seasonal art, sales information, or whatever on the non-address side, and leave the other side open for address and message. Check with the post office or www.usps.org for paper and size specs.

A thought that counts

When a letter is too long and a phone call too intrusive, try this inexpensive option: A colorful carrier for your business card, one that has space for a short message. Use a cover stock (65-lb. is good) that complements your business cards. Add a fold to the top, and this design sits nicely atop anything you need to send.

Business postcard

1 Rules: .5-pt; **Return address:** Franklin Gothic Book Condensed, 9/10-pt., align left; **Headline:** ITC Officina Serif Book, 24/24-pt., align left; **2 Label:** Space for a standard 1" × 2 ⅝" label; **3 Greeting:** ITC Officina Serif Book, 24-pt., align left; **4 Name and address:** Franklin Gothic Book Condensed, 10/11-pt., align left.

Caption card

5 Greeting: Formata Light, 14-pt., align left; **6 Name & Address:** Formata Light, 9/10-pt., align left.

Shipping label

7 Rules: 1-pt, boxes filed with K15; **Labels:** (FROM, TO, VIA) Franklin Gothic Condensed, 9-pt, reverse, align left; **Address:** Times New Roman, 12/14-pt, align left; **8 Headline:** Racer, 70-pt, align left.

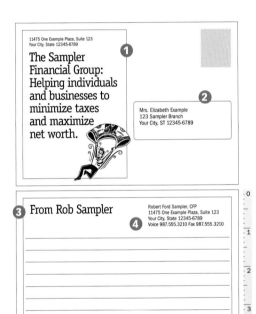

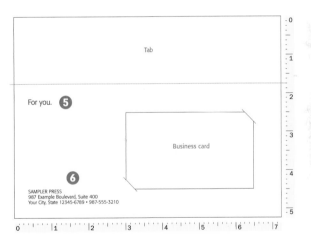

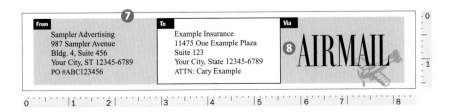

Consistency please!

Design business stationery

Business stationery is generally composed of a business card, letterhead, and a #10 envelope: Together, it's called a "system." In designing your system, your watchword should be *consistency*. Elements should be the same size on every piece, and roughly in the same arrangement to each other. Why? Because the audience's memory does not just record the color of a logo or the personality of a typeface: It also makes a note of spatial relationships. When

things are off kilter, your identity message will not get through.

Design your business card first. It is the smallest piece, so it has the most restrictions in terms of where items can be placed. The logo should be the most prominent visual element, which is achieved by floating it, in color, in a large area of white. Consider the three options on the following pages.

Name, address, and phone numbers are set in one type size on a single line. The name stands out because it's in all caps, a super-bold weight, and—especially important—is colored to match the logo. Extra blank space is used between the name and contact numbers to separate information.

Single-line specs
Logo: 5p0 wide; **Company:** 8/9 Garamond Condensed Ultra; **Address, phone:** 8/9 Garamond Condensed Light; **Name:** 8/9 Garamond Condensed Bold.

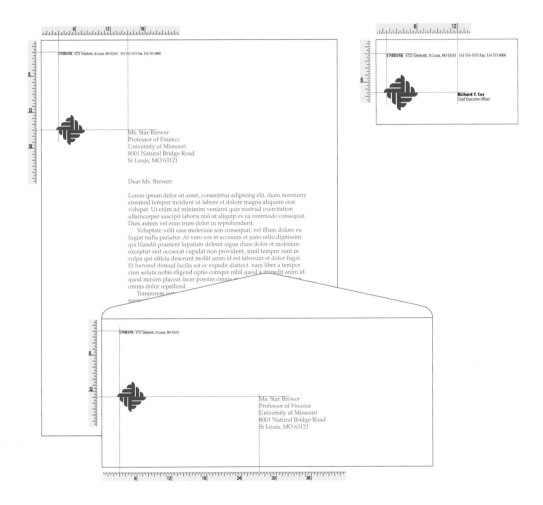

2 The big-type model

This handsome stationery makes a bigger show of the company name. Your name mustn't over-power the logo, though. Here, narrow, widely spaced letters and recessive color keep it in check. Note the same color also unites the distant (low) letterhead address with the name.

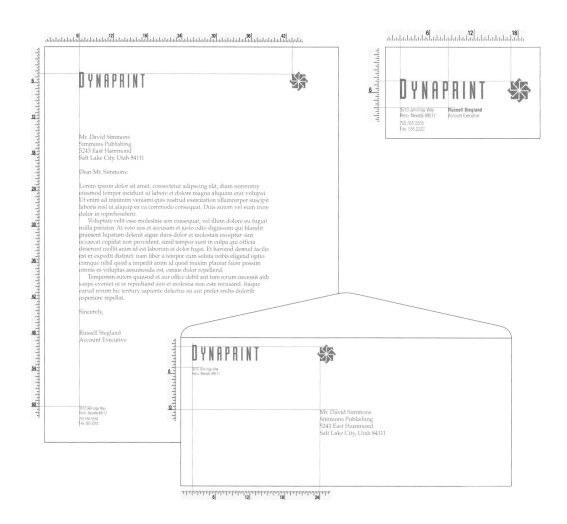

A favorite of corporate designers, different kinds of information are divided into equally spaced columns. Note subtle column shortening on the business card for fit considerations. Multiple columns give you extra places to align letter and address lines. It's clean and crisp.

Multicolumn specs
Logo: 3p6 wide; **Company:** 9/9 Kabel Ultra; **Address, phone:** 8/9 Kabel Book; Name 8/9 Kabel Bold.

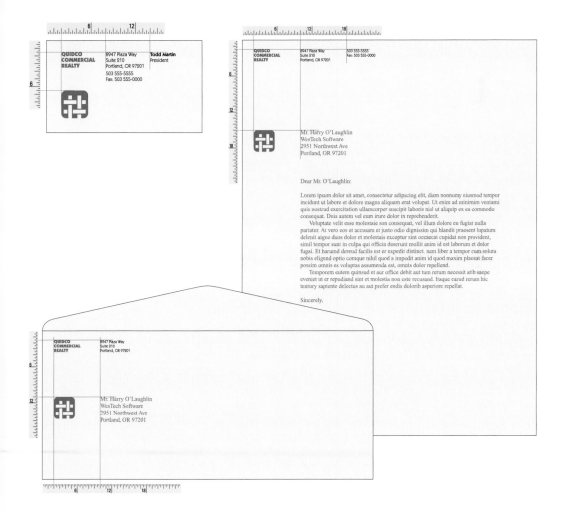

The fine art of emphasis | By Chuck Green

For those of us who hate to beat around the bush, here is a little idea with a big stick. A page stamp is a word or phrase that extracts the essence of your message. Use it large or small, top or bottom, in free space or tucked under type.

To create your stamp, all you need is a program that allows you to shade and rotate text or permits you to create a watermark. Type your text big (bold sans serif fonts are best), and add a bar to the top and bottom. Fill all the elements with a 10- to 20-percent tint of black and save the resulting image as a graphics file. Then, next time your page needs emphasis, import and place your page stamp.

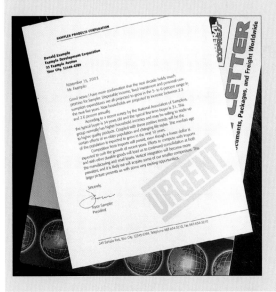

Stamp ideas:

Approved	FYI	Route
Caution	Good News	Rush
Confidential	New	Thank you
Copy	Notice	Update
Craft	OK	Urgent
Excellent	Rejected	Warning
Express		

How to set a phone number

Phone and fax numbers can be handled in a number of different ways, none of which use parenthesis. Try any of these options.

Change weight.
916 555 5634

Short dashes work.
916-555-5634

Space it out.
916 555 5634

Use a double decimal.
916.555.5634

Bullets do, too.
916 • 555 • 5634

Use short slashes.
916 / 555 / 5634

Try italics.
916 555 5634

Try a combination.
916.555-5634

Graduate space.
916 • 5 5 5 • 5 6 3 4

Change size.
916 555 5634

Make an envelope of your own

Preprinted papers are great, but none are as great as what you can make for yourself—and here's a lovely way to get envelopes in full color right from your desktop printer. It takes time to trim, fold and glue, so it's best if all you need are a few, but for that special occasion, the results are one of a kind. Find a stock image, or better, use your own camera or scanner.

1. Place and print

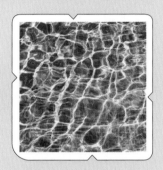

2. Fold and trim

3. Glue

The template

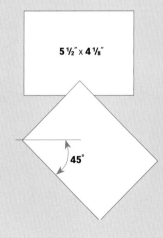

5 ½″ × 4 ⅛″

45°

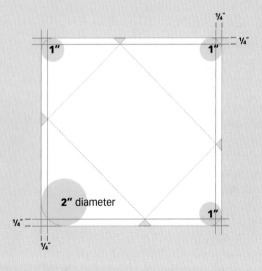

¼″

¼″

1″   1″

2″ diameter

1″

¼″

¼″

Quick—before you forget! | By Chuck Green

Gathering ideas on paper

Nolan Bushnell (the founder of Atari) once said, "Everyone who's ever taken a shower has an idea. It's the person who gets out of the shower, dries off, and does something about it who makes a difference." Great organizations rise and fall on the suggestions, dreams, and ideas of people. This pad is designed to help you leap the first hurdle—to get ideas on paper.

Create pads for everyone in your office—one for each desk, lunchroom, copy center, and reception area—anywhere you'd hang a sign that says THINK. Keep a few at home, one each in your car and briefcase. Invent incentives for participation and for results. Call it paper power—these little pads serve a purpose and send the message: *we value your insight.*

Sketch:

Sampler Industries 475 Example Ave., Suite 2

Idea pad layout
1 Subhead: Franklin Gothic Condensed, 9.5/9-pt, align left; **Headline:** Frankin Gothic Heavy, 4-pt, align left; **Box:** 20% black **2 Text:** Franklin Gothic Book Condensed, 10/11-pt, align left; **Lines:** 0.5-pt, 50% black; **3 Address:** Franklin Gothic Condensed followed by Franklin Gothic Book Condensed, 10/11-pt, align left.

Name: **2**

Date:

Subject:

Description:

1

Suggestions,
Improvements,
Dreams &

ideas!

Action:

3

Sampler Industries 475 Example Ave., Suite 200, Your City, ST 12345

- 0

- 1

- 2

- 3

- 4

- 5

0   1   2   3   4

Logos & Identity

The most successful business logos share valuable characteristics.
Here are some of the most important.

What makes a good logo?

A successful logo can't be just creative or clever. Because a logo ends up being an important guest at many occasions, it absolutely must perform and behave well no matter what.

It is a tricky balancing act, but one that you can achieve. All you have to do is consider what makes a logo effective. Make sure your design follows these guidelines.

1 | It is simple

The "too busy" logo is a roadblock to communication, so don't crowd it with stuff: green, flag, fairway, golfer, peninsula, borders, circles, curving type. It's easy to get carried away, but you'll create a stronger image with fewer pieces.

TYPEFACE: WEISS

RIVER BEND
GOLF CLUB

2 | It is bold

Fine lines make lovely illustrations but poor logos because 1) they're difficult to see, and 2) a fine line will often break up or even disappear when reproduced.

CASLON 540

FUTURA CONDENSED EXTRA BOLD

Although the two logos are rather similar, visualize them on vehicles moving through city traffic. You'd—blink!—miss the first one.

3 | It works well in all sizes

This one is often overlooked by designers who make presentations on large format paper: The logo that looks great at billboard size must also work on a business card.

TYPEFACE: VAG ROUNDED

Typically, a logo designed at a large size has too much detail to be clear when reduced. Note how the lines crowd together at left. A good solution is to build a second logo with less detail for use in small sizes (right).

4 | It is appropriate for the business

This seems like common sense, but in the throes of artistic rapture, common sense often goes out the window. Make sure the whimsical cropduster that was so much fun to draw is suitable for the client, in this case, a regional commuter airline.

Don't settle for the ordinary (let other companies be ordinary). Your company is unique—that is, it has a distinctive culture and market presence; capture this intelligently and thoughtfully.

Blah. Bravo!

Circles are strong design elements

A circle is a familiar focal point which the eye can interpret with little effort. Its soft edges are more often pleasing than those of angular squares and triangles. Cousin to the circle is the ellipse.

Avoid trendy typefaces

Unless you're in the fashion business, the type you choose for your corporate identity should still be suitable years from now. Laser printer standards—Times, Palatino, Helvetica—are always appropriate; in general, low-key is best.

Avoid extremely tall or wide logos

Odd shapes are hard to fit into common spaces—business cards, advertisements, and so forth—and as a rule they aren't as pleasing, either. A good proportion for a logo is roughly 3 units by 2 units tall, about the ratio of a TV screen (a 1-to-1 ratio also works quite well).

Too wide

Too tall

Just right

Design logo and name as a unit

If the company name will be part of the design—especially popular on signage—look for ways to integrate the two.

Here, matched colors do the job.

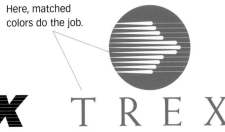

WEISS

Horizontal white lines extend to tie in the name.

HELVETICA NEUE BLACK

What's a "logo"?

There are many words flying around today, all of which relate to logo and identity design. We've isolated some of the most common catchwords to help you use the right word at the right time.

So what is a logo? It's slang for *logotype*, which usually refers to a company signature or mark. It derives from the Greek, *logos*, or *word*.

In graphic design parlance, the word *marks* properly refers to the broad group of designs that are used as corporate signatures. Marks without type are called *symbols*, but symbols used to communicate (like traffic signs and on restroom doors) are really *pictographs*.

When marks are wholly typographic, they can be *lettermarks, wordmarks,* or *monograms,* which are usually initials or abbreviations, or

logos, which may be entire words or the company name. When symbols and logos are used together, they are referred to as *combination marks.* And when any of the above are registered and protected by law, they are referred to as *trademarks.*

In publishing, many people use the words *logo* or *masthead* to refer to the publication's name on its cover, but the correct term (especially in reference to newspapers) is really *nameplate* or *banner.* And a *masthead,* or staff box, is a column of type that lists the publishers, owners, staff members, and address and phone numbers.

Tip: To be safe, use *mark* or *identity* when referring to a company's logo; use *nameplate* to refer to a publication.

Here's how to turn lively little dingbats into excellent logos and stationery.

Let's design logos!

Dingbat fonts provide a cornucopia of raw material for creating modern logos. Many dingbats are artistically excellent; all spare you much of the labor of drawing. But their biggest asset is to help you visualize by giving you something tangible to study. All can be converted to paths in a drawing program, disassembled, rearranged, skewed, rotated, scaled, colored, and otherwise altered to yield an amazing number of interesting, useful images.

The basic four steps

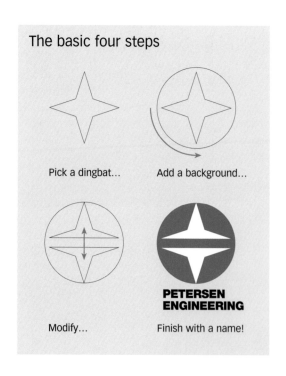

Pick a dingbat...

Add a background...

Modify...

PETERSEN ENGINEERING

Finish with a name!

Express the *intangible*...

Dingbats create *abstract* logos. Unlike pictorial logos (graphic representations of real objects), or symbolic logos (a globe, say, that signifies humankind), an abstract logo works by *suggesting* meaning. It is vague by design. This is especially valuable when:

- You're a service business whose product is intangible.
- You wish to convey intangible qualities such as strength, partnership, vision and so on.
- Your company has diverse divisions or will in the future.

An interlocking group might suggest teamwork, partnership, or cooperation. An ordered arrangement can symbolize structure or security. A flower shape might imply growth.

Overlapping objects encircling a center might imply movement, planned action, or unity. Interlocking shapes might signify connection or group strength.

Suggest the *physical*...

Many fine logos are based on physical objects. For example, to a printer a printing press is a thing of beauty, but to customers, it's a noisy, inky contraption. A printer, therefore, would want a logo that suggest the qualities of his or her press without actually revealing it.

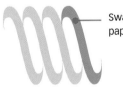
Swashes suggest paper in motion

Diamond circles suggest rollers

Pinwheel suggests fanned paper

Set an artistic stage

A background is a simple shape you draw yourself that serves as a stage for your dingbat. Many dingbats look good—even great—on their own, but others are more effective with a background. Use a background to:

- Make your logo bolder
- Give your logo a more pleasing shape
- Smooth an uneven edge
- Intensify the color
- Create dynamic tension

Use simple shapes
The best three background shapes are circles (and *minor* ellipses), squares (and diamonds), and polygons up to 6 points. These simple, symmetrical shapes keep the viewer's eye centered easily. Less effective are narrow ellipses, rectangles, triangles, and many-sided polygons, which tend to dissipate energy.

Target and define

The dingbats that most often benefit from a background are those with organic shapes, many points, or uneven outer contours. The background corrals them into a compact, visual target that's ideal for use on business cards, stationery, and commercial signage of all kinds.

A background gives *body and presence* to an airy, organic dingbat, and it transforms it into a bold business symbol.

Different shapes may look good on your dingbat: Try several before settling. Note here the corresponding corner-to-point relationship of the polygon.

Reverse and *energize*

Dingbats almost always look best light on a dark background. You'll find that reversing the dingbat makes the background dominant, which can make a dramatic difference.

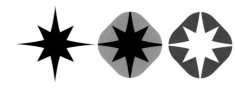

Big difference 1
Reversing dingbat turns dark spikes into a light spark.

Big difference 2
In its natural state, exuberant spines radiate outward from this dingbat's bright center. Left, a dominant background restrains the spines and yields an intriguing, vaguely dissonant, and totally different image.

Scale and reposition

Many dingbats benefit from the dynamic tension created by off-centering or rotating them. Different positions imply stability, movement, and so on. Be bold! This step needs your artistic eye.

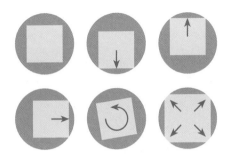

Rotate, rescale, and move your dingbat to touch every edge. You'll find each hints at something different. Resting on the bottom implies weight and stability; touching the right suggests forward movement, and so on.

Which sunburst is best?
The dingbat's size and position within its background affects what the logo communicates. Which of these sunbursts would you select?

---

3 | Create! Transformations *expand* your options...

Take it apart

The dingbat straight from the box is only a starting point. Disassemble and rearrange its parts, and you'll often find many useful images hidden inside. Some ideas:

- Separate a section
- Realign halves
- Move each section
- Rotate one or more sections
- Delete part of it

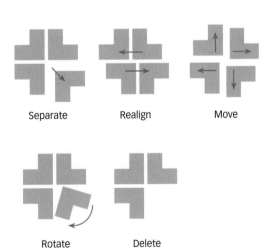

Transform one or more parts

Dingbats are generally symmetrical. Rescale and reflect one or more of the parts. Here, three good images emerge from one dingbat.

| Split the dingbat in two | Reduce the top half | Place on a background | Reflect the smaller section | Reflect both sections |

Use only *some* of the parts

Throw parts away: Individual pieces are sometimes more useful than the whole, especially when juxtaposed with a background. Look for surprises. Try these ideas.

Simply deleting half the dingbat creates a graphic sunrise.

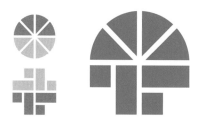

Cropping results in an abrupt and unexpectedly interesting lower edge.

Build it from separate parts

One dingbat may not be enough. Duplicate parts or whole dingbats, then cascade or rotate them. Also, create fresh, new images of your own from two or more dingbats.

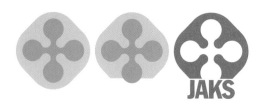

Two ways to build
Combine sections of a border font by stacking or rotating (above), or combine parts from two or more dingbats (left).

4 Add the company name

Make the name small…

Your name is what turns a logo into a business trademark. For stationery and papers that will be read at arm's length, a small, understated name has great authority.

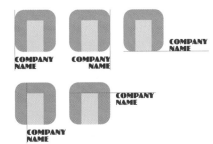

Where?
Align the name flush right or left with centers, edges, or other lines of sight. Background edges are an obvious place to start.

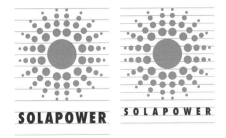

How wide?
Limit the size of the name to the width of the logo. If the name is short, spread it out. Uppercase type is usually better at this than lowercase.

…or make it big!

For a delivery truck or exterior signage, the name must be very large. At outdoor sizes, the name dominates the logo, and typestyle becomes the key design element.

Lines of sight
As before, watch for lines of sight, only this time you're fitting the logo to the name. The two most common are the ascender and x-height of the typestyle (the height of the letter "x" in a particular face).

Create a stylish, compact logo by combining a picture with your company's initial.

How to make a lettermark

In the Middle Ages, craftsmen began stamping their products with a personal seal as a guarantee of quality. Their seals became known as *trademarks* and have been popular ever since.

Early trademarks were highly decorative, with elaborate drawings and busy lettering. Although their purpose remains the same, their appearance has evolved. Modern trademarks are streamlined—the illustration is reduced to a silhouette, and the company name is set in simple type.

The illustrated letter, or *lettermark*, is an especially effective type of trademark—it's stylish, compact, and easy to complete.

Here's how to make an effective lettermark.

BEFORE DRAWING...

The letter is the foundation of your lettermark. Its shape and proportion will govern everything that follows. Look at it carefully. As a rule, you'll place your illustration within its largest open area. Plan your graphic so its proportion matches this space.

Quick start

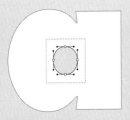

1. Type your letter
Pick a typeface and in a drawing program, type your letter and then convert it to a path. Select its counter (the hole) and delete.

2. Make your graphic
Make (or find) a simple graphic that illustrates the product or services of your company—in this case, a tropical fish store. The graphic needs very little detail; it's the silhouette that's important.

3. Combine
Position your silhouette to replace the missing counter. Note that although the graphic is larger than the counter was, the letter retains its original character.

---

1   What to draw: Look for pictures that tell a story

Start with a real object

If your client has a tangible product, draw it first. If it has many products, try several; each will say something different. If the product is actually a service (like a motel), try objects from the environment, such as this cactus or teapot.

If a literal image doesn't work, try symbolism

A symbolic image brings to mind a desirable but intangible characteristic of a company—strength, for example. We're not looking for abstraction or hidden mystical revelation here; the best symbols are pictograms (like restroom signs) or everyday objects.

Real objects make the best symbols. Birds can represent peace; the light bulb, a great idea; a bull, strength or power.

Draw the profile
Logo graphics are meant for quick identification. Illustrate the object in its most recognizable view.

Use as little detail as possible
Elaborate pictures are pretty but out of place on a lettermark. Use only what's needed to make your graphic identifiable.

Too fancy.　　　What is it?　　　Just right.
It doesn't
take much.

Using lines? Limit yourself to one line weight
Lines are racy but can quickly appear detailed and overworked. The solution: Use a single line weight throughout.

Lines are equal; spaces between are equal.

Keep the outline simple
The teddy bear shown below is easy to "read" when it's big, but it looks like an ink blot at letterhead size: Its silhouette is too busy. A solution was to render only teddy's head. Watch for similar conditions in your design.

WHICH TYPEFACE?

When picking a font, choose a very bold sans serif or slab serif style. These usually retain their character when combined with an illustration. Avoid extremely condensed bold faces: Their tall, thin counters are too restrictive for replacement graphics.

Ee
FUTURA EXTRA BOLD

Ee
AACHEN BOLD

Ee
MEMPHIS EXTRA BOLD

Ee
FRUTIGER ULTRA BLACK

Ee
BODONI POSTER

EE
MACHINE

Remove the counter and place your graphic in the largest open area of the letter. Usually, you'll want to make your illustration larger than the counter it replaced.

You won't always find them, but look first for points of alignment: Your lettermark will be strongest if the letter and graphic pull in the same direction. Note above how the tulip appears to be part of the *P*, not added on.

Place for legibility
Your letter will be clearest if you position your graphic to follow its natural contours.

Nice pens, but what letter are we looking at?   Much better!

Avoid this
When placing graphics, work with, not against, the natural shape of the letter.

Try these ideas

Repeat a graphic (below left) or make a whole word from lettermarks (below right).

A trail of ants is more repulsive than just one critter. A technique like this requires a very clear letter.

Note the naked *I* in this playful lettermark name. As a rule, avoid putting graphics into letters that lack open area.

A wordmark is a logo without pictures, and it's hard to believe it's so easy!

How to design a wordmark

A logo without symbols or pictures is called a *wordmark*, and it is easier to make than any other kind. Wordmarks are the most widely used of all logos: In fact, many of the largest companies use them.

Like any logo, a wordmark is a symbol of something. Before you begin, take time to consider what that *something* is. What is the company you are trying to represent? Is it a thing or a person? Does it manufacture a product or provide a service? Who is its market? You want these answers because as you work, you'll find the lure of new and interesting graphics can

lead you into blind alleys—it's easy to wind up with an enchanting logo that has little to do with the company's actual needs. The more you know about the company, therefore, the less likely you'll wander.

In this article, we'll design a wordmark for Berington Insurance. The principles demonstrated here can be applied to any logo.

Quick start

1. Select a typeface and set the company name.

2. Adjust the size and alignment. Here we've made one word large and centered the other words.

3. Enclose the words in a box traced around their perimeter. Fill.

4. Embellish with ruled lines—and you've designed a fine logo on short notice.

1 Select a typeface

In a wordmark, typestyle plays the key role. Your first step is to fish one from an ocean of choices. Some guidelines:

When set in type, a name sends an explicit and implicit message. The explicit is what's actually said; in this case, Berington Insurance. The implicit is in how it's dressed, or the tone of its voice. What you are looking for is the interaction of the two.

Let's try one:

BERINGTON

The implicit message always depends on the context. In this setting, Mr. Berington might be an insurance specialist for military families. To the general public, however, he could be mistaken for a shipping company. Let's try another:

BERINGTON

The chiseled face used here imparts the sense that this guy will be in business for years to come. Now let's change the explicit message.

AUTO REPAIR

Uh-oh. That same reassuring typeface now says something different: *This mechanic is going to be very expensive.*

That's what we mean by interaction.

The best way to evaluate type is to set the company name with every font in your library and have a look. You'll gravitate toward the showier typestyles, so pay attention to the plain ones. Why? They're often more forceful. For example, Caslon won't stand out on a page of specimens:

AaBbCc

Yet set in uppercase with added letterspacing…

BERINGTON

…it looks positively regal, and it carries the clout that befits its stately bearing.

Be aware, too, that a single line of type often does not reveal enough: Its implicit message will be altered by other factors in your design. For example:

BERINGTON

is set here in Lithos, a typestyle with funky, Greek, African overtones. This attitude, though, demands funky typesetting. In a specimen catalog, its attributes are very easy to miss.

We settled on Odeon Condensed, a super-squished, industrial-grade typestyle, for Berington. *Insuranc*e can be set in the same typestyle or another can be selected. Pay attention to the interaction of faces. Usually, you want the words to read *as a unit*. In this example, you'll adjust type sizes and make use of your program's *Force justify* feature to align both words to the right and left margins. Here are some possibilities:

BERINGTON INSURANCE

The single font solution
By chance, *Berington* has the same number of letters as *Insurance*. Setting both words in the same typestyle at the same size creates instant alignment.

PARKS
INSURANCE

What if the words are different lengths?
If you choose the single-font approach for a company with unequal-length words in its name, reduce the size of the longer word to achieve alignment.

BERINGTON
INSURANCE
FRUTIGER ULTRA BLACK

Use a contrasting font
Set the second word in a typeface chosen for contrast; in this case, that means bold and squat. Adjust the type size until it aligns with both edges of the dominant word.

BERINGTON
I N S U R A N C E

Increase the contrast
For more contrast, increase the difference in size but keep the two words aligned right and left. To do this, *Force justify* the second word.

BERINGTON
I N S U R A N C E

Spread out the type
Adding space between letters can create a luxurious feel. This is especially true with condensed typefaces. If you spread both words, put additional leading between them.

3 Enclose in a shape

Now look at your words and evaluate the shape they form (try squinting at the grouping). Next, draw a box around the perimeter of this shape— or part of the shape—and fill. This works with both single- and multiple-word logos. Here are three approaches:

The shape gives the type stage presence and makes the words stand out on the page. By outlining the type perimeter, the type structure is also emphasized.

This principle applies even if the type is staggered. Note how the top and bottom lines of type are aligned. Drawing around the shape of the type enhances the dynamic look of this logo.

Shape can be a tool for emphasis. For example, draw a shape around one part of the type arrangement, which makes the enclosed section stand out from the rest of the logo. Note how the type outside the shape has been re-justified to the box edges.

4 Add and align rules

Rules add the polish and give your logo style. Because they emphasize structure, they can draw attention to the company name. Sometimes, you'll use rules simply for decoration.

When adding rules, *always align them in some way with the type of graphic shape*. This is not only neater, it also unifies type and shape into a single powerful logo.

When adding rules to your logo, sample different kinds of alignment. Here, the rules align with the edges of the type, framing the name.

In this case, the company name is emphasized by three horizontal rules. By highlighting the type, the name seems to stand out from the graphic shape.

Heavier rules impart a feeling of strength. Because they align horizontally, they help the reader see the two words as a single unit.

Rules aren't always needed; some wordmarks look fine without them.

Set a name, then try all of these techniques!

INDUSTRIA SOLID

ONYX AND COPPERPLATE 33BC

Make exotic shapes
Because the type arrangement determines the graphic shape, experiment with unusual ways to set the company name. Stagger the size of the letters in a word (left), or join type along a circular path (below left).

Try unfilled shapes
The Book Mark and Bennett logos look better with the shape left unfilled. If you choose the "open look," experiment with different line weights for the shape.

TIMES BOLD AND TIMES ROMAN

CENTURY SCHOOLBOOK AND HELVETICA BOLD

Make handsome logos from standard laser printer fonts
You don't need a large type library to create good-looking logos; the wordmarks above and below were made using standard laser printer fonts. There is one weakness with standard laser fonts, though: The bold weights are sometimes not very bold and therefore don't create much contrast. Solution: Create contrast by increasing the size difference between words.

BAUER BODONI

COPPERPLATE 33BC

Emphasize a company's products or services
Rules and bars are powerful pointing tools. Use them to call attention to part of the company name to emphasize its products or services. Note here that instead of running the full length of the name, the rule underlines only the part requiring special notice.

CORVINUS SKYLINE

SHELLEY VOLANTE SCRIPT

Add parts to a shape

If an outline isn't stylish enough—and sometimes it isn't—start adding stuff! Top, we attached semicircle ends and embellished the resulting notched corners with dingbats (use only one kind of dingbat per logo). This is the kind of technique you make up as you go.

Dantés' swashy typestyle was dropped into a less restrictive oval shape. Rules were added strictly for show. Try different line weights (above right).

HELVETICA BOLD

Repeat a shape

A shape can be used more than once. Try one per letter, or one per word.

CHARLEMANGE BOLD

Create wordmarks for companies with long names

If you have a client whose company name is practically a sentence, this type of wordmark is excellent. Decide which part of the name to emphasize, make it big, and *Force justify* or center the remaining words for alignment and balance.

Creating an initial-mark?

When designing an "initial-mark," the type arrangement is simpler but the concepts still apply: Just treat the initials as a complete word.

Initial logos have always been popular, but they have limitations. For one, a single initial conveys very little information about the company it represents. Solution: Set the full company name next to the logo.

M.N. HOLDEN REALTY

BODONI POSTER   ULTRA CONDENSED SANS

Although only initials, the shapes of both logos are still determined by the type. Note how initials combine with the full company name into a forceful logo (above left).

TIMES NEW ROMAN

Although you're not justifying whole words, don't forget about alignment when applying rules, bars, and dingbats. It will offer the same unifying results.

BAUER BODONI   FUTURA EXTRA BOLD

Single-letter initial-marks present a monogrammed logo. Try these on personal stationery.

Inside your name is a real logo—and finding it is as basic as one-two-three!

Discover the logo in your name

Boca Technology Group, Inc., is an engineering consulting firm whose products include esoteric computer peripheral products. Boca is a company of engineers whose first priority is not logo design. Its logo does not convey the sense of a cutting-edge company nor its employees, high-octane business brains.

But visual image should be part and parcel of a company's name. Consider Coca-Cola's swish and Nike's swoosh: Who wouldn't recognize these symbolic marks? Such imagery is important on a local scale, too, among engineers and the company's clients. It can bestow on a viewer the sense that the company is stable, brainy, and can be trusted.

So how do you design a logo—especially when you have other work to do? How do you create an image that conveys a sense of discipline, excitement, and vision? What follows is a simple, effective way, using just type and a simple shape. Turn on your computer, select an ordinary typeface (these examples use Helvetica), and follow along.

BEFORE

The goal in logo design is to change an ordinary word into a visual *object*. There are many ways to do this, but in every case you must pay attention to *kerning*. To kern means to adjust the space between pairs of letters for a better fit. As a rule, you'll tighten a setting overall, then adjust the space between odd-fitting pairs.

Each of the styles on this page has characteristics that will be affected by the meaning of your word and the shape of its letters. Set as many as you can, then have a look—your unique name will acquire a character all its own.

Boca
Boca

Pay attention to kerning for a better-looking logo.

LOWERCASE

boca

UPPERCASE

BOCA

Case

As a rule, words set in lowercase tend to appear casual, friendly, and warm. Uppercase is commanding and authoritative; it's the case of inscription on buildings.

LIGHT

BOCA

HEAVY

BOCA

Weight

Light type—especially super-tight as shown here—tends to feel airy and clean, informal and decorative. Heavy type is steady, solid, and muscular: It can easily dominate a space.

NARROW

BOCA

WIDE

BOCA

Width

With their tight focus, narrow styles suggest a no-nonsense operation. Wide styles are expansive, modern, airy.

TIGHT

BOCA

LOOSE

B O C A

Spacing

Closely related to width, tight or overlapping type creates a sense of focus and urgency. Loosely spaced type feels panoramic, like the powerful, horizon-spanning vistas of the movies.

2 | Define its space

A word's *voice* comes first from its style but then from its relationship to the space around it. The next step, therefore, is to draw a space—a simple shape—against which your word can interact. As you move it around, what you'll see is a whole range of expressive characteristics. Here are eight common positions:

By reversing the type, the eye perceives the two elements as one object rather than a word in a box. A shape the same proportion as the word (above) reinforces the word.

Up
Modern, buoyant, light; type at or near the top suggests growth.

Left
Conservative, moored, stable but not dull—left says "dependable."

Front
Powerful, dominant, forward-thinking, this logo wants to be first.

Vertical
Radical—makes you work to read it. It's decorative and rebellious.

Down
Grounded, stable; type near the bottom is traditional, elemental.

Right
A logo on the move, a name on the right suggests progressive.

Back
The background greets you first. Understated, very authoritative.

Angled
Unstable but energetic; decorative; background shape is critical.

If your name has another part of a descriptive subhead, its position relative to the main word will affect the rhythm and balance of your logo, as well as how the name is perceived. As a rule, this second part should be set much smaller; try one-sixth the size of the larger word. Where should it go? Watch primarily for *edges* and *points of alignment.*

Think in columns

Think of your logo as having columns—one aligned with each letter—and place your subhead on any one.

As the subhead moves from the conservative leftmost position (above left) to the more energetic and unconventional right, it also shifts the balance rightward. As you work, keep an eye on both expressiveness and visual aesthetics.

These columns exist no matter what the shape.

Every word has unique and often unexpected angles that can be used for alignment, from a horizon (far left) to the angled *A* (left).

Because it draws the eye to its center, the circle is the most focused of all natural shapes.

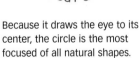

In the triangle and diamond, the subhead relates not to the word but to the shape that contains it.

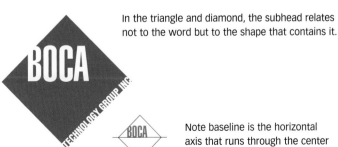

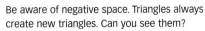

Be aware of negative space. Triangles always create new triangles. Can you see them?

Note baseline is the horizontal axis that runs through the center of the diamond.

Here's how to create a good look out of nothing—just a name on a shape—but there's a secret.

Design a name

Who needs fancy artwork? Good design is the happy result of words, shapes, colors, and other basic elements in harmony. Simple shapes—rectangles, ovals, polygons—have real, expressive presence. A rectangle, sharp-edged and pointy-cornered, says something that a circle, round and soft, does not. So it's easy to create a good look out of nothing—or at least what seems like nothing: Set a word, add a shape behind it, then color! Or start with the shape. Or the color. The secret is to get all three elements *saying the same thing*. Here's how:

---

1 | Rectangles

A rectangle is the most stable shape—flat, firmly on the ground, motionless. A rectangle is the shape of *structure*—the walls of a building or monument, for example. Dark, substantial colors are full of black and feel solid, connected and dependable. Uppercase type is stately. The overlap adds a light counterpoint appropriate for a restaurant.

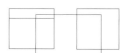

THE
MAPAKADOS
MEDITERRANEAN GRILL

WADE SANS LIGHT

2 | Circles

Light, delicate pastel colors are full of white and convey fragility and vulnerability, even infancy. Pointy-cornered rectangles won't do here; what's needed are oval shapes that are gentle. The type, too, should *whisper*—lowercase, ultra light, and white, which recedes.

HELVETICA NEUE ULTRA LIGHT

3 | Triangles

Angles are the most exciting forms, full of energy, motion, and instability, which is why you see them on skateboards and not on corporate stationery. Amp up the volume with an angular typeface. Riotous colors—bright secondaries, mainly—are seen in nature in flowers, tropical birds, and fish.

ROXY, ATLAS

Typestyle, color, and a dash of flair say volumes about your company.

Monogram logo conveys character

Historically, a monogram was a monarch's treasure—a hallmark bearing the most revered icon of all—the royal seal. It said little, but spoke with immediate recognition.

A few centuries later, monograms still command attention. Sure, the royal seal is gone, but the monogram's simple, quiet elegance remains—the elegance of a name, an initial, and the visible voice of character.

The easy-to-make monogram shown in this article is a great example. To make it, first you'll draw a circle, an initial, and a name. What's exciting are the endless ways in which typestyle, value, and small embellishments can then be combined to convey exactly what you want. Dress them in the costume of royalty, and they

speak of the privileged. Bathe them in a spotlight of smoky blue, and they fill the imagination with slow, swaying jazz. Center them on a stage of texture and accent, and they whisk us somewhere else. Here's how to do it:

1 Draw a circle

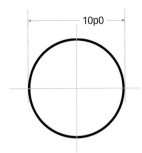

Draw a circle with a 10-pica diameter. Set the stroke to 3 points. Crisscross two ruler guides and center the circle at the guide intersection.

Now start thinking about the image you want to send out. Is it sophisticated, casual, traditional, sporty, futuristic? And what typeface expresses it best?

2 Set your initial

Your initial is the focal point of the monogram, and it's fun to experiment with typestyles. What you are looking for is *expressiveness*—your choice may be ornate, blocky, rough, classic, bold, whatever. Pick one you like—we're using Snell Roundhand—and for now set it in 120-point.

3 Center and scale

Center your letter by eye and scale it to fill up the circle. Make it big; it's all right to touch or even overlap the circle like we've done here. At this point it's hard to tell what will look best, so just get it in the ballpark, and we'll fine-tune it later.

4 Set your name on a path

Set the company name on a 11-pica diameter circular path, similar to what's shown here. To start, we've used 16-point centered type, in all caps. Since it's much smaller than the initial, the font should not be ornate or detailed; ours is Charlemagne.

5 Space the letters

Increase the letterspacing until you are pleased with the results. To extend a too-short name, you might try adding a bullet between letters, or repeat the name, or use a more extended font.

6 Add an outer circle

Draw an outer circle as shown here, so the type is spaced evenly between the circles.

Before moving on, take a look at the whole thing; you'll now have a better idea if the type is the size you want, if the spacing pleases you, and so on. Adjust if necessary.

These spaces should be equal

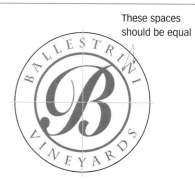

7 Color

Monograms look great in just one or two colors. Pick a deep, rich main color—burgundy, grape, midnight blue, forest green, charcoal. The second color, if you use one, should be light: a pale screen of the first color; a neutral cream or gray; or a complement. Here, the inner circle is a tint of the outer. White type gives the illusion of three colors.

8 Embellish

Lines, texture, and pattern can help to symbolize the company's business. Use them to conjure up mental pictures. Here, horizontal lines bring to mind old engravings, or are perhaps reminiscent of the grain in the wood barrels, and turn the monogram into a wine label. Old-world dingbats fill space artfully, easing the "jump" between words.

Artistic guidelines

The example illustrated on the previous pages balances many variables. When you create a monogram, you must also balance proportion, typestyle, and color.

Proportions

A monogram is like a target: The eye is drawn to the center (**1**), then led outward (**2**), because its elements are scaled from large to small. How large should they be? How small?

Avoid typefaces that leave gaps

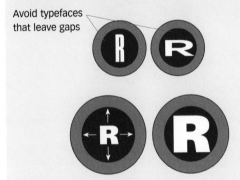

This   Not this

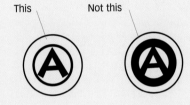

The initial

Fill up the circle. For your initial, pick a typestyle that's as wide as it is tall, You want it to fill the space and look substantial and secure, not to float or appear weak. Steer clear of condensed or extended typefaces, which in a circle leaves big gaps.

Lines

Take special care. Line weight should be no heavier than the initial, and preferably lighter.

The name

Set it midsize. As a rule, your circular type should be one-seventh the size of the initial. For "period" designs and other special pieces, you might try it larger (far left), but go easy: Too big and it tends to compete, too small and it's unreadable (left).

Type

Typestyle is the costume your initial wears to express your company's character: playful, stately, flamboyant, confident, whatever. Use the visual language of type to convey your company's spirit.

Working basic
The basics are sometimes ideal and always worth a look. This logo is set in Palatino, a standard laser font.

The initial
Make it expressive. For bright results quickly, start with decorative headline fonts. Look first for something energetic, blocky and bold, or ornate. Sometimes a solution is obvious: a swashy script initial, say, for a fancy hotel. But try everything. Chances are you'll be surprised by interesting results from some unlikely choices.

The circular name
Start with the same typeface. Try first setting the circular name and initial in the same typeface; this establishes immediate uniformity and is often the strongest choice. Always set the circular name in uppercase; the up and down shapes of lowercase make for an uneven, weak appearance (above right).

Too elaborate   Much better

1 uniform   **2** uneven   **3** repeat name

Name uneven? Too short?
Even it out. Words of uneven lengths, such as Laurelwood Books, can be set in uniform letterspacing (**1**) or uneven (**2**). Set a too-short name twice (Al Dente) or three or even four times (**3**).

Make sure it's readable
Keep it simple. If your initial typestyle is elaborate, you'll need to set the circular name in a different, simpler font. Look for contrasts. Try serif/sans serif, script/serif, or bold/light combinations. Keep in mind that your choice must be easy to read at small sizes.

Color

Monograms look unusually good in black and white, but it's color that draws attention and expresses character more than any other element. Color is why, as you read this text, you can feel the pull of Zorro's solid red pizza box (previous page). Color can also affiliate a monogram with a nationality, school, sports team, and so forth.

Use solid color for boldness
Bright, solid color without screens has the broadest range of use. This is ideal when printing on uncoated paper on which screens could easily plug up.

Two colors
A dark color for body, a light color for accent.
Monograms are beautiful in two colors. To find the most expressive ones, it will help to browse your draw program's color libraries. Look first at the burgundies, grapes, midnight blues, forest greens, and charcoals. The most vivid monograms are predominantly dark. Select a light second color for *accent*—a pale screen of the first color, creams, grays, or complements. As a rule, avoid making the light color dominant, which weakens the effect (above right).

Tints
Tints make the most of one color. Tints soften and give dimension to one-color logos. Since tint values are most obvious in shades of gray, work in black and white first. Alternate values from the center out: dark, light, dark, light (above left), then apply those same values to a dark color (above right).

Companies of every kind sign their names with letters that link.

Design your own ligature

There is probably no artistic style more intuitive than blending two or more letters into one. The result is a letterform called a *ligature*. Ligature means *to tie*. Letters that are tied make a compact signature perfect for companies that are known mainly by their initials.

Ligatures are fun to design. They require no special drawing talents, just an ordinary sense of rhythm and an interest in putting puzzles together. Some letters, you'll find, link naturally while others do not. Some link in one typestyle but not another. Others link in lower case but not upper. Some can be doctored to link, others cannot. And some can be fooled into linking.

As children we got acquainted with our own initials. As designers, we must get acquainted with different letters. What follows are techniques, ideas, and advice to help you line up as many different letters in the most expressive ways you can.

Many letter pairs form natural links. By *natural* we mean that the letters have identical parts or complementary shapes that fit hand in glove. Let's begin with the easiest letters to link—those that have adjacent matching strokes, like NR, AV, and HK, and similar strokes, like UR and AB. These are linked by using the matching stroke for both characters.

Natural letter pair links

Conjoined letters make a new character, a true ligature. Two colors put emphasis on one letter or the other, a good way to handle an acronym in which the second letter is the more important.

FUTURA BOLD

Try changing case...
The lowercase alphabet is much different from uppercase, and many letters that do not link in one will link in the other. As a rule, lowercase ligatures impart a less formal, more playful image.

HELVETICA NEUE ROMAN   RUSSELL SQUARE

Try changing font
Similarly, letters that don't link in one typeface may link in another. Try lots! Typefaces that would be much too showy for everyday use often make excellent ligatures.

ADOBE GARAMOND

HK are an ideal pair; each letter is distinct from the other but their adjacent stems are identical. Link by removing either stem and abutting the letters.

Lowercase Uppercase
An uppercase *I* can't merge with anything—its body just disappears. But a lowercase *i* has the advantage of its distinctive dot and can merge with many letters. Here, a lowercase *i* has been doctored to link with an uppercase *M*.

The *i* occupies the space of a stem, which makes a great two-color ligature. For one color, the *i* must be separated to the left.

GOUDY SANS

Angled to vertical

Angled letters usually link beautifully to vertical letters. The easiest way is simply to cut the angled letter in half.

Watch for unplanned letters!
Some letter pairs that have matching strokes should not be joined. While the L fits the T perfectly, the odd result looks like we've invented a new letter. An attribute of a good ligature is that its letters read as individuals even after being joined.

SERIF GOTHIC HEAVY

SPRING

Almost identical

Pairs like UR share not-quite-identical stems, yet flow naturally together. To link neatly, you must usually sacrifice some parts; here, the R gave up a foot, the U a serif.

Curved to vertical

The more decorative the typeface, the more easily dissimilar strokes can be linked. Even a curving stroke can replace a vertical. You need gentle curves for this to work, though—circles won't do.

HELVETICA NEUE EXTENDED   AMERICAN TYPEWRITER BOLD

COPPERPLATE

GLYPHA

Top crossbars

A few letter pairs share top crossbars. These link so obviously they can appear to be merely kerned tightly. The way to avoid this impression is to add an outline (above left) or pattern, or alternately, use a serif typeface and share the serif (above right).

Mid-letter crossbars

Uppercase ABEFHPR all have mid-letter crossbars that can be connected with a little help: Just cut the letter apart and s-t-r-e-t-c-h the bar. Key is to keep the letterforms distinct and not deform them, either. You can do this by separating the letters with two colors, or for a one-color ligature by making a gap in the intersecting stroke.

Letters can be linked in many other ways. They can be looped, overlapped, bridged, filled, outlined, and more. Every letter pair is special and can usually be made to link in more than one way. Try these:

Will it stand up?

A good ligature is well balanced and rests on solid footing. To achieve this, it may help to think of it as a physical object. Here R and P have been linked in a logical but unstructured way. If this ligature were a physical object, it would tip over. This inadvertent lack of stability sends a subliminal message about your company.

Remove a stroke

Here, a phantom stroke hints at what's not there. This is particularly effective with Modern typestyles such as Bodoni that have extremely thin strokes: Just remove one leg and move the letters together.

CENTURY OLD STYLE

Remove part of a stroke

Letters with angled and overhanging arms—FKTVWXYZ—benefit from this technique, which is especially good in serif typestyles. The illusion is that of a stencil; the line is interrupted, yet our eyes "fill in" the missing part.

Follow the white line

Create the illusion of attachment. Rather than abut letters (below right), leave a gap, then make a flowing centerline that draws the eye smoothly around.

FUTURA BOLD

An entertaining ligature unique to the T, disconnect one arm and attach it to its neighbor.

The C and B don't naturally link, but C, like the semi-closed G and S, can be opened. Remove and redraw the C's curling arms, then open the closed B by pulling up its vertical stem.

ADAMS
SMITH

BERNHARD MODERN

ADOBE CASLON   FUTURA EXTRA BOLD

Add box   Reverse letter   Tint to soften

Crop!

Your intrigued reader will linger for valuable moments on this design. Crop away the bottoms of your letters, and the viewer's eye must complete the image. Add the company name or other horizontal graphic to span the gap.

Reverse the field

Attach a matching color box to your letter, then reverse the second letter out of the box. This is especially effective with three-character acronyms (top right). White is most vivid but is sometimes too stark; a tinted reverse is softer.

Interlocked

Not a ligature in the strictest sense because its letters remain whole, interlocking nevertheless unites letters so tightly they function as one graphical unit. Excellent with circles, particularly effective with beautiful, cursive script.

Woven

Masterful weaving of adjacent curves yields a very polished look. Right, lap one letter atop the other, cut and reassemble. Different typefaces require different kinds of fussing.

What's in the negative space?

Negative space is the empty area in and around your letters: It has shape and presence and always affects the viewer's perception. Negative shapes are often trivial but sometimes take on familiar forms—note the plump P (top right)—that rise to an active role in the design. They can add energy that's available in no other way and turn ordinary work into great work. Watch for negative shapes.

Build Bridges

This technique works when nothing else will: Abut your letters, then conceal the junction with a simple graphic, line, or series of lines and shapes.

GOUDY SANS BOLD

Bright yellow dots mask the junction of the two letters. In this case, the dots just lay on top.

ITC KABEL DEMI

Here, barely touching letters are brought together by playful shapes and colors. Although completely different, they feel so similar that the eye reads the letters as a single image.

BAUER BODONI

The diamond does double duty—joining the letters and helping to form the shape of the R.

GILL SANS EXTRA BOLD

See the similarities!

Some letters appear to link not because they physically connect but because they look alike. Watch for similarities. Here, changing typefaces turn the *a* into an almost mirror image of the *b*, making an interesting visual form.

Inset

One letter enclosing another works for only a few pairs but can be quite effective. The key is to use a font with no thicks and thins so the letters fit without uneven gaps.

BODONI

What is that? A leaf? Make sure your counterless letter is clear.

Replace a space with a letter

Some letters are big enough to hold others inside. Replace the enclosed space (called the *counters*) of one letter with another letter. You can mix font, case, style, and size. The byword is *readability*. Use a background font that's clear in silhouette and a foreground font that doesn't compete.

GOUDY SANS BOLD

Color the negative spaces

Some stubborn letters just won't link. So link their background instead. Put letters in a box and color the negative spaces; the result can be a fun, harlequin-like pattern with a lighthearted energy.

FUTURA

Overlaid

If letters that are overlaid still appear separate, pull them together with a common fill or stroke. Here, a graduated, green-to-blue fill turns two letters into a single object.

You buy them separately, but art and type are two sides of the same coin—
and there's magic in making them work together. Here's how they relate.

The art and type tango

Today, tens of thousands of professionally drawn images are available to everyone for pennies each. Type, the classic high art, is being given away by some companies almost for free.

Let's put these tools to work—together. It's typical to think of art and type separately: Art goes *here*, type goes *there*. But as a rule, they're more effective together than apart. This means they operate in the same space—overlapped, side by side, stacked, interwoven, and so on. This allows the characteristics of each to rub off on the other, adding up to a "word image" that's greater than the sum of its parts.

The easiest art
A lot of useful artwork comes hidden in the form of dingbats–visual odds and ends such as dots, stars, arrows, curlicues, and other doodads. The most common are Zapf Dingbats, which come standard on nearly every laser printer.

1 Overlapped

Proximity is the key...

Proximity is what turns individual letters and artwork into useful logos. Bring letter and graphic close, closer, close enough to overlap, and you create a simple, artful icon.

ADOBE GARAMOND   Close...   closer...   kiss!

Proximity has many expressions. While the spade above can stand alone, the swash at right cannot. Here we overlapped the *M*, then added an embellishment. The swashy dingbat resembles a swaying frond; two circles were all it took to suggest the breezy tropics.

FUTURA, GENEVA

Picture atop the name...

What's the Cookout Company's specialty? The image answers the question without saying a word.

BLOCK T REGULAR CONDENSED

Note that the fish faces the company name. This is how to keep the two connected. If it were swimming the other way, you'd wonder if you should, too.

2 Side by side

Big graphic, small word...

Create a boardroom look of authority by making the graphic object prominent and understating the typeset name. More big companies do it this way than any other.

A diamond shape creates an arrow-like point of tension. As you work, be sure to rotate, reflect, and skew a graphic; you'll often be surprised by good solutions you could not have otherwise foreseen.

HELVETICA NEUE EXTENDED HEAVY, ADOBE GARAMOND

Big word, small graphic...

A simple graphic can expertly convey who you are and what you do. In this case, replacing just the apostrophe is enough to create an unmistakable air. Look for ways to replace punctuation marks or even whole letters.

Note the monochromatic color scheme of yellows and golds. Colors that are similar to each other—reds and violets, greens and aquas—always harmonize readily, and, more important, the eye identifies them as belonging together. Note, too, the "reverse case" treatment of the type. The larger and more important word—*fifi's*—is set in lowercase, while the

FUTURA BOLD, FUTURA LIGHT

smaller word—STATIONERS—is in uppercase. You can get excellent results from such unexpected contrasts. Try a contrast of very large but very light type against very small and bold.

---

3 Stacked

Sandwich...

Stacking a letter atop a graphic is the classic way to create decorative initial caps, monograms, and handsome logos, simply.

BAUER BODONI BOLD

When combining letter and graphic, watch for the interplay of values—that is, the relative darkness and lightness of the objects. To illustrate, the light *E*, right, is lost in the dark ornamentation. This can be solved by adding a dark background (right center), which subdues the ornamentation and allows the letter to stand out. To achieve similar separation but without the background, tint the ornament lightly (far right).

CENTURY EXPANDED

See through!

A complete merging of text and graphic—both occupy the same space yet are fully visible. Useful for glass, plastic, haze, gauze, motion, dreamscapes, and so on.

HELVETICA NEUE EXTENDED BOLD

Words *tell* and pictures *show* at a glance.

Why have words *here* and pictures *there*? Instead, put them together to double their impact. Verbal and visual combined are greater than the sum of their parts.

Same size, same shape, same place.

Make it bounce or move.

Words move, pictures punctuate!

Sophisticated

At right, a different object sends a sophisticated message; the soccer connection is obvious but wordless. What's cool here is that comprehension is not instant; it requires the reader to *linger* for valuable moments, soaking your message in.

What creates such a strong illusion of depth? It's that as an object on the ground moves toward you, it appears bigger and lower in your visual field (go outside and look at cars). To mimic that, make your photo bigger and lower than the letter it replaces.

Proud sponsor, West Central Flame

Three kinds of contrast
Word color determines voice and emphasis...

Same Cup color unifies

Similar Beautifully subtle

Different Cup stands out

Can't decide on that one perfect graphic? This surprising technique uses them all!

Design a playful, multi-image logo

The traditional logo consists of a name and a single, carefully crafted graphic, uniformly applied to every company document. But here's a design with a refreshing twist: a logo made of three, four, five, or more graphics scattered around a neatly set name and address. It's a cheery style suitable for any subject from auto repair to flowers to sportswear. And it's fun to make, especially if you enjoy composition more than drawing, because its artistry is in its *arrangements*. Every piece is different; the arrangements from business card to letterhead to even a T-shirt can change to fit the shape of the space—which makes for lots of expressive possibilities. Here's how it is done.

Design with silhouettes

Silhouettes are the easiest, most versatile, most available kind of artwork because you can make them yourself from a wide variety of original material—photos, line art, halftone drawings— and they appear to have come from the same pen. Look for a clear profile, then simply trace and fill.

A logo that's all over

What's more ordinary than garage tools? They could be dull as dishwater, but when scattered thither and yon they convey an appealing sense of lightness and freshness. What makes this work? Watch for two things. First is *similarity*. Whether you use three images or ten, choose images that share one or more characteristics such as subject, style, or color. Second is *uniformity*. The artistic arrangement can (and often must) vary to fit the space—spread out on *this* piece, compact on *that* one—but the remainder of the layout should be uniform from piece to piece (note text blocks and left-hand margins). This uniformity gives the material its disciplined, orderly appearance and allows the exuberant imagery to take center stage.

Type specs
Name: ITC Machine
Address: Helvetica Neue 55 Roman

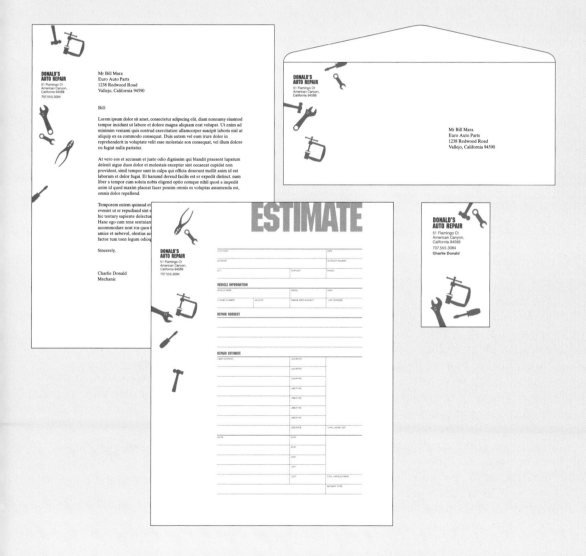

1 Establish a simple foundation

The basic elements of a stationery system are business card, letterhead, and envelope. Although these have different sizes and proportions, they serve a related purpose, and your goal is to have them look like they belong together. To give this showy logo freedom to move, the margins and supporting elements must remain rigidly in position. Here's how to pull this off:

DONALD'S AUTO REPAIR
51 Flamingo Ct
American Canyon,
California 94589

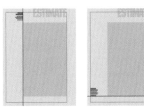

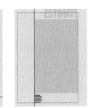

Set your type in one block
First set your type in one plain block, aligned left or centered (1). Two typefaces are plenty; they should be simple and fairly small—an 8-pt. address is usually big enough. This block will be the same size on all your pieces, so fit it to your business card first.

Place it in a corner
Place your text block in a corner the same direction from the edge of every sheet. (Corner can mean the real corner [2] or a corner formed by the outside margin and the edge of the live matter [3, 4].) A scattered logo takes up a lot of room, so at least one of your letterhead margins—usually the left—should be very wide.

Say it with photos

Photos make excellent scattered logos, especially if they're of familiar objects. Key is to use images that are visually simple—that is, that have few lines, plain textures and a clear silhouette. Color may be simple, too. The flowers in this example have complex lines, shapes and textures, but each makes a nice, big spot of color. Flowers have another asset: They're so familiar our brains *think* they're simple.

2 | Scatter your artwork purposely

As you lay out your images, pay attention to *weight*, *balance*, and *lines of sight*. Sort your objects loosely into groups. Each group will have the visual weight that can balance or off-balance the others. Begin by placing a main group in some open space, then place single objects or small groups on the periphery. Note the text block itself has weight and is an important part of your composition. You'll find that many objects such as the screwdriver and wrench are directional like pointers, and the eye will tend to follow them subconsciously. These have extra value! Use their pointing characteristics to move the reader about the page. On the T-shirt design below, the three flowers encircle the name and point to it.

TIP

Look for these natural pointers that can be used to direct the eye toward important information.

Group...   isolate...   add more groups

Natural pointers

Many objects are natural pointers; their shapes move the eye subconsciously in one direction or another. As a rule you want these objects to point *into* the page, *toward* the message, as shown here.

Balance

Every element on your page, including text, has visual weight that can be used to balance or unbalance your design. Keep the center of balance near the center of the layout. A heavy group near the center can be counterbalanced by a light group near an edge.

Sales & Forms

Basic guidelines can improve even dull forms.

Guidelines for a good layout

A crucial link in the readability chain is *page composition.* The elements of page composition include column width, white space, and the location of text within the space. They also include typographic *contrasts,* that is, shifts in tone and pace conveyed by changes in type style, weight, and size. Proper handling of these elements can have great and beneficial effect on even the most ordinary documents. We'll illustrate with a standard disclosure statement handed out by banks to mortgage loan applicants.

Where's the trick?

In the unfamiliar terrain of home-financing lingo, can you think clearly enough to grasp what a disclosure statement is telling you? Although it's written in plain English, it *looks* dense and difficult, a visual impression that alone can render a nervous applicant frustrated, suspicious, and defensive.

In real life, our conversation is full of animation, punctuation, and pauses in interest and emphasis. To communicate easily and well, we want to convey these natural and expressive qualities in print. This is done with composition and changes in type style, weight, and size.

BEFORE

DISCLOSURE STATEMENT

NOTICE TO MORTGAGE LOAN APPLICANTS: THE RIGHT TO COLLECT YOUR MORTGAGE LOAN PAYMENTS MAY BE TRANSFERRED. FEDERAL LAW GIVES YOU CERTAIN RIGHTS. READ THIS STATEMENT AND SIGN IT ONLY IF YOU UNDERSTAND ITS CONTENTS.

Because you are applying for a mortgage loan covered by Real Estate Settlement Procedures Act (RESPA) (12 U.S.C. Section 2601) you have certain rights under that federal law. This statement tells you about those rights. It also tells you what the chances are that the servicing for this loan may be transferred to a different loan servicer. "Servicing" refers to collecting your principal, interest and escrow account payments. If your loan servicer changes, there are certain procedures that must be followed. This statement generally explains those procedures.

TRANSFER PRACTICES AND REQUIREMENTS

If the servicing of your loan is assigned, sold, or transferred to a new servicer, you must be given written notice of that transfer. The present loan servicer must send you notice in writing of the assignment, sale or transfer of the servicing not less than 15 days before the date of the transfer. The new loan servicer must also send you notice within 15 days after the date of the transfer. Also, a notice of prospective transfer may be provided to you at settlement (when title to your new property is transferred to you) to satisfy these requirements. The law allows a delay in the time (not more than 30 days after a transfer) for servicers to notify you under certain limited circumstances, when your servicer is changed abruptly. This exception applies only if your servicer is fired for cause, is in bankruptcy proceedings, or is involved in a conservatorship or receivership initiated by a federal agency.

Notices must contain certain information. They must contain the effective date of the transfer of the servicing of your loan to the new servicer, the name, address, and toll-free or collect call telephone number of the new servicer, and toll-free or collect call telephone numbers of a person or department for both your present servicer and your new servicer to answer your questions about the transfer of servicing. During the 60-day period following the effective date of the transfer of the loan servicing, a loan payment received by your old servicer before its due date may not be treated by the new loan servicer as late, and a late fee may not be imposed on you.

COMPLAINT RESOLUTION

Section 6 of RESPA (12 U.S.C. Section 2605) gives you certain consumer rights, **whether or not your loan servicing is transferred.** If you send a "qualified written request" to your loan servicer concerning the servicing of your loan, your servicer must provide you with a written acknowledgment within 20 business days of receipt of your request. A "qualified written request" is a written correspondence, other than notice on a payment coupon or other payment medium supplied by the servicer, which includes your name and account number, and your reasons for the request. Not later than 60 business days after receiving your request, your servicer must make any appropriate corrections to your account, and must provide you with a written clarification regarding any dispute. During this 60-day period, your servicer may not provide information to a consumer reporting agency concerning any overdue payment related to such period or qualified written request.

DAMAGES AND COSTS

Section 6 of RESPA also provides for damages and costs for individuals or classes of individuals in circumstances where servicers are shown to have violated the requirements of that Section.

DISCLOSURE STATEMENT

❶ *Notice to mortgage loan applicants: The right to collect your mortgage loan payments may be transferred. Federal law gives you certain rights. Read this statement and sign it only if you understand its contents.*

This statement tells you about your rights
Because you are applying for a mortgage loan covered by Real Estate Settlement Procedures Act (RESPA) (12 U.S.C. Section 2601) you have certain rights under that federal law. *This statement tells you about those rights.*

"Servicing" refers to collecting your principal, interest and escrow account payments.

If your loan servicer changes, there are certain procedures that must be followed. *This statement generally explains those procedures.*

❷ ## Transfer practices and requirements

❸ **You must be notified in writing**
If servicing of your loan is assigned, sold, or transferred to a new servicer, you must be given written notice of that transfer.

❹ **You must be notified *before* the transfer**
The present loan servicer must send you notice in writing of the assignment, sale or transfer of the servicing not less than 15 days *before* the date of the transfer.

You must be notified *after* the transfer
The new loan servicer must also send you notice within 15 days *after* the date of the transfer.

❺ *A notice of prospective transfer may be provided to you at settlement (when title to your new property is transferred to you) to satisfy these requirements.*

Some delays are acceptable
The law allows a delay in the time (not more than 30 days after a transfer) for servicers to notify you under certain limited circumstances, when your servicer is changed abruptly. This exception applies only if your servicer is fired for cause, is in bankruptcy proceedings, or is involved in a conservatorship or receivership initiated by a federal agency.

❻ *Transfer notices must contain certain information:*

They must tell you the exact date of transfer
They must contain the effective date of the transfer of the servicing of your loan to the new servicer.

They must make a way to answer your questions
They must contain the name, address, and toll-free or collect-call telephone number of the new servicer, and toll-free or collect-call telephone number of a person or department for both your present servicer and your new servicer to answer your questions about the transfer of servicing.

Your on-time payments must be honored
During the 60-day period following the effective date of the transfer of the loan servicing, a loan payment received by your old servicer before its due date *may not be treated by the new loan servicer as late, and a late fee may not be imposed on you.*

Complaint resolution

Section 6 of RESPA (12 U.S.C. Section 2605) gives you certain consumer rights, *whether or not your loan servicing is transferred.*

Your servicer must acknowledge your request within 20 days
If you send a "qualified written request" to your loan servicer concerning the servicing of your loan, your servicer must provide you with a written acknowledgment within 20 business days (about four calendar weeks) of receipt of your request. A "qualified written request" is a written correspondence, other than notice on a payment coupon or other payment medium supplied by the servicer, which includes your name and account number, and your reasons for the request.

Your servicer must make appropriate corrections within 60 days
Not later than 60 business days after receiving your request, your servicer must make any appropriate corrections to your account, and must provide you with a written clarification regarding any dispute. During this 60-day period, your servicer may not provide information to a consumer reporting agency concerning any overdue payment related to such period or qualified written request.

Damages and costs

Section 6 of RESPA also provides for damages and costs for individuals or classes of individuals in circumstances where servicers are shown to have violated the requirements of that Section.

Type makes the message visible

Divided into conversation-size parcels, our suspicious document, it turns out, is actually good news. Several useful techniques are involved: **1** an obvious and strong beginning; **2** clear topic markers; **3** simple statements of fact repeated in **4** brief explanations; **5** visual changes in tone; and **6** visual shifts in direction. The result mimics natural conversation: It's easy to read and understand, which inspires confidence in the reader. This is always good for business.

What's changed? Text size and leading are the same (10/12), but everything else is new.

Wide margins

White space is an underrated asset, and it's free. Wide margins are like fresh linen: They set an open, inviting table. Set margins before anything else: One inch all around and 1½ inches on the left is a good place to start. If you can get more space, take it.

Medium-length lines

Medium-length lines are the easiest to read. Shoot for about 50 characters per line—in 10-point type, that's about 17 picas. This is more art than science—not all typestyles are the same—but it's better to be a little short than too long.

Typographic contrasts

Two type families are better than one; select a light serif for text and a bold sans-serif for contrast. Use the sans-serif style for small but vivid flags that summarize each point. Use oversize *serif* type for major headlines; this is how to convey the authority of prominence without shouting (undignified) or clashing with the subheads. Use italics (not bold) to change your emphasis or tone of voice, and set each section apart from the rest with empty space—in this case, a half line.

Offset to the right

As a rule, a text field offset slightly right has more energy and presence than one that's centered. It also has room for three-hole punching.

Sparkling and compact, photocoupons have full-page appeal
at a fraction of the price.

How to design photocoupons

The compact photocoupon is an excellent place to hone your advertising skills. It's small, inexpensive, colorful, and efficient, not to mention easy and gratifying to work with. Because it has only one photo and few words, you can experiment freely and judge the results immediately.

A coupon is by nature a *response generator*. It silently invites the reader to take an action. A photocoupon works by taking full advantage of this built-in response stimulus. It makes an

excellent small ad in a newspaper or magazine. It also works as a postcard or business reply card. As part of a larger ad, a photocoupon creates a lively center of interest without the expense of a full-page image. It's slick.

Confined to such a small space, you'll find that all components—photos, words, and type—play a bigger-than-usual role. They must be visually and verbally concise.

Here's what to pay attention to:

1   Write two headlines

Key to designing a photocoupon is to think of it as an ad, only briefer. This means paying attention to the headlines. You can often double the impact of your headline by writing two, each evoking a slightly different flavor. Key is to keep them separated visually, which can be done with typographic contrasts or simple distance. Here the two are separated by typestyle and color: The superbold black face (Futura), although smaller, has the same visual impact as the headline above it, which recedes because it's white. Unless you have a "house" typestyle, always take your type choice clues from the image itself. Here, the towering typeface (Willow) amplifies the effect of the overwhelming snow.

The coupon is the ad

Packing a full page of advertising punch into roughly a 4×5-inch space, a photocoupon yields more bang per inch than anything else in print. The treatment here is the most straightforward; blanket the background with a single, full-bleed photo. Since it must be written on, you need a light or neutral image. Our example has been simplified for clarity. Keep in mind, though, that a coupon's strength is in its simplicity. Photo and headline should carry the ad; you may want to add a sentence of text and your address in fine print, but no more.

2   Small photo carries the page

This is opposite the usual arrangement; instead of saturating a whole page with an expensive, full-size photo, color only the coupon (right). Much cleaner on newsprint, this also creates an ad with not one but two clear focal points—headline *and* coupon—doubling your chances a busy browser will stop and read.

3 | Say the same thing twice

When speaking orally, there's a time-tested rule for addressing an audience: Tell them what you're about to say, then say it, then tell them what you said. Each telling, of course, should be a little different, but the value is in its repetition. This works just as well in print. Note here the headline and coupon text say the same thing in different ways. You can hardly overuse this technique: Just keep in mind your audience is like you—busy and preoccupied—and repeat what you said.

Translucent coupon is part of the picture
Sophisticated but also more demanding, here a lightened corner of the photo defines the coupon. This technique is handsome anywhere, but it's especially useful when your photo is too dark or too busy to write on (or even read on). It's also handy when a photo isn't the right shape, or when your ad is larger than coupon size.

Everything is relative to the photo.
When designing a photocoupon, your photo is the show: It attracts the eye, defines the subject, sets the tone, and prepares the viewer to read, all in an instant and usually subliminally. In the presence of a strong photo, typography *always* takes a supporting role. What's interesting is that the photo, in turn, brings type to life. Atop a photo, typefaces you'd overlook as dull when set alone (above, City) take on vivid new impact. You'll find it's like doubling your type library for free.

4 | Bridge the gap

This photo reaches across the coupon and links it with the body, thereby doing two jobs at once. This is especially useful when you want a large photo, or when your photo is vertical. Note the two widely separated headlines; they create two zones of interest that work off each other—you read one headline, form an impression, then the other. What's interesting is the heads could be swapped and work just as well. Typographic contrasts are key.

5   Toss a photo atop the coupon

Here we're inviting conference attendees to an event as our guests. Even if there's no actual ticket involved, the presence of the ticket says to the viewer, "You're in." What's important to note is that the copy doesn't mention a ticket: We simply use the ticket's visual air to set the stage for our invitation. Its cockeyed placement makes the most of its familiarity. The ticket is just lying about, the way you'd see it on a table-top. Note the extreme typographic contrasts between the blocky, superbold headline (Egyptian) and the elegant script subhead (Snell Roundhand).

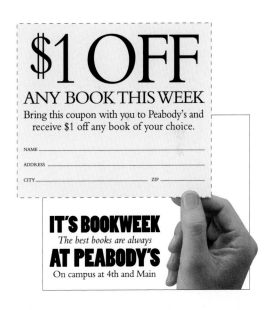

6   Build the coupon around the photo

Here's the opposite approach: We started with the picture, then built the coupon to fit it. Pictures of people (faces first, hands second) are the most compelling of all images and draw viewers no matter where they're used. Note the hand is not part of the message; it's here strictly for its expressiveness. (Do you use your hands when you talk on the phone? Like that.) At the bottom, unusual two-in-one head-lines give you two messages for the price—and space—of one. The ad's visual sophistication comes in part from its typographic contrast— a classic, light serif (Bembo) plays against a massive, hand-hewn superbold (Poplar). Dashed coupon border is hairline weight.

This technique is a great use for those photo-clip-art libraries that feature single objects selected for their descriptive visual imagery—hands in various poses, a ticket, an alarm clock, a pencil, a lifesaver, a hat, and so forth. The strength of these photos is that they bring to mind familiar situations. They will be most effective if you use them incidentally rather than literally; in other words, use, say a megaphone not to sell megaphones but to stand in for something like cheerleading or moviemaking. It could also be a visual metaphor for voice or volume.

Square plug-in modules make handsome, organized pages in a hurry. | By Chuck Green

Snap together a great catalog

A good catalog is a 24-hours-a-day selling machine. It's as effective as your leading salesperson, as knowledgeable as your top buyer, and as organized as your best administrator. It captures on paper everything that's good about your business.

But, boy, can it be tough to build. Material comes from a thousand different sources. There are products and accessories of every shape, size, and description; and hundreds, even *thousands* of codes, styles, photos, prices, updates, specials, new models, delivery times, return policies. It's a triumph just to get it on paper. How does one even *think* about design?

How about the easy way—with a catalog built entirely of compact modules that snap neatly into a handsome grid. Not only does it look great, it also goes together fast. Plug-ins simplify the process of organizing your design basically by removing the ambiguity. With clearly designated slots for everything, what starts out as a jumble of words and pictures can be smoothly transformed into neatly packaged "information parcels" to be mixed and matched in any way you choose. And just as important, the same structure that's so easy to build is unusually easy for your reader to navigate. Let's have a look.

OFFICE FURNITURE OUTLET

Sensational Seating

How much time do you spend in your office chair? Lorem ipsum dolor sit amet, consectetur adipiscing elit, diam nonnumy eiusmod tempor incidunt ut labore et dolore magna aliquam erat volupat. Ut enim ad minimim veniami quis nostrud exercitation ullamcorper suscipit laboris nisl ut aliquip ex ea commodo consequat.

B · Sensible Seating—Task Chairs

This task chair gets our vote for the perfect computer chair. Lorem ipsum dolor sit amet, consectetur adipiscing elit, diam nonnumy eiusmod tempor incidunt ut labore et dolore magna aliquam erat volupat.
Ut enim ad minimim veniami quis nostrud exercitation ullamcorper sus cipit laboris nisl ut aliquip ex ea com.

CODE	ITEM	REG.	NOW
1000	Swivel	$000	$000
2000	Swivel, tilt	$000	$000

Bestseller!

E · The 7700 Series Seating

Adjusting to the challenge at hand. Lorem ipsum dolor sit amet, cons ectetur adipiscing elit, diam nonnumy eiusmod tempor incidunt ut labore et dolore magna aliquam erat volupat. Tempor sunt in culpe qui officia des erunt mollit anim id est laborum et dolor fugai.

CODE	ITEM	REG.	NOW
1000	Swivel	$000	$000
2000	Swivel, tilt	$000	$000
3000	Multi-task	$000	$000
4000	Guest	$000	$000

A · Sensible Seating—Executive Chairs

Why do they call it "sensible seating?" Lorem ipsum dolor sit amet, consec tetur adipiscing elit, diam nonnumy eiusmod tempor incidunt ut labore et dolore magna aliquam erat volupat.
Duis autem vel eum irure dolor in reprehendrit in voluptate velit esse molestaie son consequat, vel illum dolore eu fugiat nulla pariatur.

CODE	ITEM	REG.	NOW
1000	Low-back	$000	$000
2000	High-back	$000	$000

NEW!

C · 5301 Executive Chairs

Put form and function to work for you. Lorem ipsum dolor sit amet, consect etur adipiscing elit, diam nonnumy eliuet dolore magna aliquam erat volupat. Lorem ipsum dolor sit amet.

CODE	ITEM	REG.	NOW
1000	High-back	$000	$000

D · The 3100 Series Seating

This series of chairs was designed by HON customers. Lorem ipsum dolor sit amet, consectetur adipiscing elit, diam nonnumy eiusmod tempor incidunt ut labore et dolore magna aliquam erat. Ut enim ad minimim veniami quis nostrud exercitation ullamcorper suscipit laboris nisl ut aliquip.

CODE	ITEM	REG.	NOW
1000	High-back	$000	$000
2000	Mid-back	$000	$000
3000	Guest	$000	$000

What's makes a great chair?

If you sit in your chair more than a few hours a day, it should have, at a minimum, these important features:
1. Padded seat and back
2. Swivel
3. Tilt and tilt tension control
4. Pneumatic seat height adjustment
5. Adjustable, padded arms
6. Adjustable back height
7. Glides suited to the floor surface

Design an office that works well and looks good.

A well designed space is comfort-able, it helps the people within it to be more productive, and it reflects your organization's style.
Lorem ipsum dolor sit amet, consectetur adipiscing elit, diam nonnumy eiusmod tempor incidunt ut labore et dolore magna aliquam erat volupat.
Ut enim ad minimim veniami quis nostrud exercitation ullamcor per suscipit laboris nisl ut aliquip ex ea commodo consequat. Duis autem vel eum irure dolor.
In reprehendrit in voluptate velit esse molestaie son conse quat, vel illum dolore eu fugiathu la pariatur. At vero eos et accusam et justo odio dignissim qui blandit praesent lupatum deleinit aigue duos dolor et molestais exceptur sint occaecat cupidat.

F · Everyday Seating

Is your chair as comfortable at the end of the day as it is at the beginning? Lorem ipsum dolor sit amet, consec tetur adipiscing elit, diam nonnumy eiusmod tempor incidunt ut labore et dolore magna aliquam erat volupat.
Ut enim ad minimim veniami quis nostrud exercitation ullamcorper sus.

CODE	ITEM	REG.	NOW
1000	Clerical	$000	$000
2000	Operator	$000	$000
3000	Designer Stool	$000	$000

We use it ourselves!

H · Solutions Seating

Does this look like an inexpensive chair? Lorem ipsum dolor sit amet, consectetur adipiscing elit, diam non numy eiusmod tempor incidunt ut lab ore et dolore aliquam volupat.
Ut enim ad minimim veniami quis nostrud exercitation ullamcorper sus cipit occaecat cupidat non.

CODE	ITEM	REG.	NOW
1000	High-back	$000	$000
2000	Low-back	$000	$000
3000	Guest	$000	$000

G · ComforTask Seating

Price, comfort, and durability—what more could you ask. Place your text in this position. To achieve the same look, choose a similar font and duplicate the size, spacing and alignment settings.
To match the overall page design, duplicate the positioning of each.

CODE	ITEM	REG.	NOW
1000	Swivel	$000	$000
2000	Swivel, arm chair	$000	$000

We are ready to fill your order! Call 212-555-1234

Would it make your day to know that someone is waiting by the phone to hear from you? We are.
Your OFO representative is ready to take your call between 9 & 5 EST Monday through Friday.

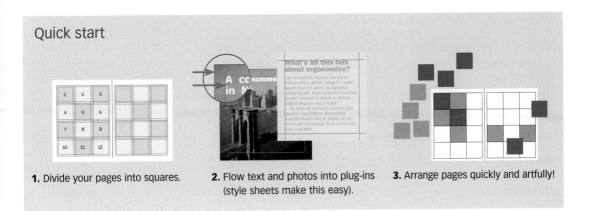

Quick start

1. Divide your pages into squares.

2. Flow text and photos into plug-ins (style sheets make this easy).

3. Arrange pages quickly and artfully!

Snap together a great catalog **143**

Plug-ins organize pages into uniform, easy-to-read bites...

Key to the plug-in catalog is to design everything in squares. There are picture squares and text squares; some are a little of both. If one square isn't enough, you can connect two or more in a row. For best looks and easiest assembly, stick to the format. Headlines are one size, body copy another, and so on. Pictures always bleed at the edges; text always begin at the upper-left margin.

Our catalog uses six different plug-ins, although for your catalogs you may have to think up some of your own. Some ideas:

Keep your irreplace-
ables super-safe
Page 22

Picture plug-ins illustrate your products. Small code letter matches corresponding text plug-in. Direct *sell lines* (shown) and buzzwords like "Our favorite!" add zest.

D · The Safe Cabinet

Where do you store your most important records? They belong in the Safe Cabinet. Lined with asbestos-free, flame-retardant insulation. Withstands temperatures of up to 1700°F for up to one hour. Resists impacts equivalent to a 30-foot fall. Lifetime warranty.

CODE	ITEM	REG.	NOW
1000	2-drawer, letter	$000	$000
2000	4-drawer, letter	$000	$000
3000	2-drawer, legal	$000	$000
4000	4-drawer, legal	$000	$000

Text plug-ins describe your products. For easiest assembly, you can modulize these descriptions. Start with the product name, add an inviting lead-in, one or two primary benefits, any important ingredients or materials, an item code, suggested retail price, your catalog price—whatever's pertinent.

OFFICE FURNITURE OUTLET

Sensational Seating

How much time do you spend in your office chair? Lorem ipsum dolor sit amet, consectetur adipscing elit, diam nonnumy eiusmod tempor incidunt ut labore et dolore magna aliquam erat volupat. Ut enim ad minimim veniam quis nostrud exercitation ullamcorper suscipit laboris nisl ut aliquip ex.

Title plug-ins introduce each section. Small text at the top repeats your name; big headline presents the product category. Note the high contrast white on black.

A cool summer
in NYC.

Accent plug-ins are for *atmosphere,* not sales. Look among stock photos for images that represent your industry, local landmarks, or whatever.

What's makes a great chair?

If you sit in your chair more than a few hours a day, it should have, at a minimum, these important features:
1. Padded seat and back
2. Swivel
3. Tilt and tilt tension control
4. Pneumatic seat height adjustment
5. Adjustable, padded arms
6. Adjustable back height
7. Glides suited to the floor surface

Information plug-ins show up randomly. A foolproof way to fill leftover space, they offer useful tidbits such as "How to plan your work area" or "Wood veneer versus solid wood." Indispensable.

**We are ready to fill your order!
Call 212-555-1234**

Would it make your day to know that someone is waiting by the phone to hear from you? We are. Your OFO representative is ready to take your call between 9 & 5 EST Monday through Friday.

Action plug-ins prompt the reader to take action. Repeat at the same place on every page, usually the lower-right corner. A series of similar photos, clip art, or even a repeating color creates a running theme.

2 Set up your grid

The squares of our model grid… aren't quite. There's extra room at the top for a running header of name, address, and phone, which is vital for every page of any catalog.

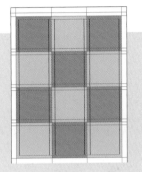

Document setup
Page: Letter size, double-sided, facing pages; **Margins:** Inside, Outside, Bottom, 3p6, Top, 5p0; **Column guides:** 3; **Space between:** 2p6; **Drag horizontal ruler guides:** (from top of page) 2p3, 3p9, 17p6, 18p9, 20, 32p6, 33p9, 35, 47p6, 48p9, 50, 63p9. **Drag vertical ruler guides:** (on each page, from center of spread) 2p3, 17p9, 33p3, 48p9.

3 Define style sheets

If you've never used style sheets, now is the time to learn. Nothing eases the toil of repetitive formats as swiftly or completely. The styles shown here duplicate our model exactly; as you set them up, pay attention to the details, especially *case, indents,* and *space after.* (Delete existing styles first.)

| Style | Type | | | | | | Paragraph | | |
Name	Base on	Next	Font	Size	Lead	Case	First	Align	After
1 Body	No style	Same	Franklin Gothic	9	10.5	Norm	1p0	Left	0p0
2 Body First	Body	Body	Franklin Gothic	9	10.5	Norm	0p0	Left	0p0
3 Eyebrow	Body	Same	Franklin Gothic	10	10	Caps	0p0	Left	0p7.5
4 Listing Title	Body	Same	Franklin Gothic	6	10.5	Caps	0p0	Left	0p0
5 Listing	Body	Same	Franklin Gothic	8	10.5	Norm	0p0	Left	0p0
6 Title	No Style	Body First	Franklin Gothic Heavy	37	31	Norm	0p0	Left	0p0
7 Headline Large	Title	Same	Franklin Gothic Heavy	25	23	Norm	0p0	Left	0p0
8 Headline Medium	Title	Same	Franklin Gothic Heavy	15	14	Norm	0p0	Left	0p3.6
9 Headline Small	Title	Same	Franklin Gothic Heavy	9	10.5	Norm	0p0	Left	0p3.6
10 Picture Tag	Title	Same	Franklin Gothic Heavy	9	11	Caps	0p0	Ctr	0p0

Cropping photos

Few photos come out of a camera ready to print. Most must be cropped to suit the designer's purpose. Cropping is how to:

- Remove unwanted objects
- Center—or offset—the subject
- Enlarge a detail
- Highlight similarities or differences
- Make side-by-side comparisons
- Add drama or excitement
- Fit a space better

When your goal is selling merchandise, cropping is especially important. Tips:

Remove unwanted objects
If the subject is among unwanted objects, simply crop them out. If more than one object is being pictured, crop so the key image is centered.

Highlight similarities
Three products are sized the same and centered. This makes them seem most alike—that they're all receptionist chairs, for example.

Highlight differences
Three similar products are centered but sized differently; this heightens their differences—shapes, fabrics, armrests, and so on.

Enlarge a detail
Crop tightly, then enlarge for a close-up. If a product is available in, say, two trim styles, this is how to compare them.

4 Place

Place your text cursor in the upper-left inner corner of a square (right) and type, selecting styles as you go. If you've done it right, the finished plug-in will be a single text block, neatly aligned and spaced.

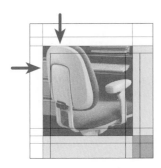

Photos, tints, and other backdrops always bleed to the outer margins of a square.

5 Arrange plug-ins in many ways to create pages for every occasion…

A plug-in can be a single square or a group of several. It can be tall, wide, or simply big. Its shape should be square or rectangular, never stairsteppy. As you arrange your pages, keep in mind that all but the covers are viewed as two-page spreads, so work on them together. Place title plug-ins in the upper left, action plug-ins in the lower right. A checkerboard (right) is easy and holds a lot, but you'll get better results with a less predictable pattern. Readers like variety. Try enlarging one or two modules, or lengthening a few. Stagger some. Plug-ins can be stacked, slid, and combined in many ways to suit the photos, the text, and your marketing needs.

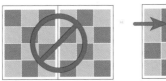 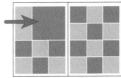

Above left, a checkerboard is orderly but repetitive. Provide an eye-catching point of entry by disrupting the checkerboard with a large plug-in (above right).

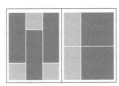

Mix and match nearly any combination. As a rule, place photos to the outside, text to the inside, title plug-ins in the upper left, action plug-ins in the lower right.

Stagger
Wide or tall modules dramatize features or simply fit the shape of the photos. Staggering images and text keeps the reader engaged.

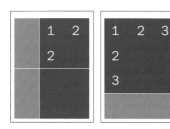

Get big
Use oversize photos to highlight important products, specials, whatever—and provide visual relief, too. Scale your photos up into 2×2 or 3×3 grid squares. If your text doesn't fill all the space, remember you can always fill single plug-ins with product tips or images.

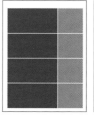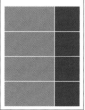

Stack neatly
Stacking identical modules yields a page that's neat as a pin. Photos go to the outside, text to the inside. For  double- (or triple-) width text modules, divide the text into square blocks (left).

OFFICE FURNITURE OUTLET

Our elegant cheap seats

To us, cheap is a badge of honor. Lorem ipsum dolor sit amet, consectetur adip scing elit, diam nonnumy eiusmod tem por incidunt ut labore et dolore magna aliquam erat volupat. Ut enim ad mini mim veniami quis nostrud exercitation ullamcorper suscipit laboris nisl ut aliquip ex ea.

A

It's stackable

B

A · GuestStacker™ Seating
Special events require special seating. Lorem ipsum dolor sit amet, consectetur adipscing elit, diam nonnumy eiusmod tempor incidunt ut labore et dolore.

CODE	ITEM	REG.	NOW
1000	Stack chairs	$000	$000

B · ComforTask™ Seating
Here's proof that an inexpensive chair can be remarkably comfortable. Lorem ipsum dolor sit amet.

CODE	ITEM	REG.	NOW
1000	Swivel, pneumatic	$000	$000

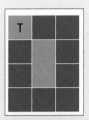

Create an island

If you have lots of photos with short descriptions, try floating the text in the center of the page and surrounding it with visuals.

Overlay small atop large

For an especially sophisticated effect, flow a single large photo across one or two pages, then overlay it with several photo or text plug-ins (place the overlaid images atop empty or uninteresting areas of the photo). For higher contrast, lighten the large photo.

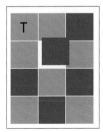 

Move outside the grid

Because the plug-ins conform so precisely to the grid, anything that doesn't fit stands out. Shift a plug-in to one side and up slightly so it appears to float above the page. Rotate a plug-in 15 degrees or so to draw attention to it. These techniques are fun and very effective—but use them sparingly: Too much of a good thing will just clutter your design.

In addition to product pages, your catalog needs
pages that help the reader navigate its contents.

A smoother cover

This proven technique makes the most of the grid: Fill
the cover with a big photo, then overlay two, maybe
three, product shots and a title square. Highlight the grid
with white lines. This works with most products and
almost always yields good results.

The back cover

The back cover of your catalog
should sell just as hard as the front.
The only difference is that you must
set aside a grid row for the mailing
label, the bulk mail indicia, and the
return address.

Note here the action plug-in slides
up a row; high-contrast title plug-in
has slid from top left to bottom.

The introduction

Use the page just inside the front cover to get your reader oriented. Note here the text plug-in is 1×4 and reversed white on black. It can cover prices, policies, company history, and should include a table of contents. Fill the remainder of the page with a photo that plays on the theme of your catalog.

The order form

The order page duplicates the introduction page, but a form replaces the photo. The form is one item of text not confined to plug-in size. If you want the customer to remove and return the form, be sure to limit the information on the opposite side to nonessentials such as sales items.

Here's a recipe for subtle selling. | By Chuck Green

Create an infomark

This "cookbookmark" is one part convenience, one part information, and one part marketing message—a simple, subtle way to advertise your products and services.

Your version might include a conversion table; a collection of industry terms or abbreviations; a list of pertinent phone numbers; or a generic tool such as a ruler or calendar. Make it useful enough and your customer will keep it, use it, and remember it.

Bookmark specs
1 Headline: Adobe Caslon Regular 40/34-pt., align left; **2 Ornament:** Adobe Caslon Ornaments, 24-pt., align left; **Body text:** Franklin Gothic Book Condensed, 12/14-pt., align left; **Name, address and hours:** Franklin Gothic Book Condensed, 10/12-pt., align left; **3 Table head:** Adobe Caslon Regular, 10/12-pt., align left; **Table subhead:** Adobe Caslon Regular, 9/9-pt., align left; **Listing:** Franklin Gothic Book Condensed, 8/9-pt., align left; **Lines:** 0.5-pt.

Tools for cooking and fine dining from Sampler Gourmet

 Sampler Gourmet has been a purveyor of fine glassware and china, imported and domestic cooking tools, and professional-quality small appliances since 1970. Keep this bookmark in your cookbook and call us with your culinary questions.

Sampler Gourmet Ltd.
12345 Example Row
Your City, ST 12345-6789
987-654-3210 Fax 987-654-3210
Open 9 A.M.–9 P.M. Mon.–Sat.

Measurement CONVERSIONS

DRY	pt	qt	pk	bu
1 pint (pt)	1	$^1/_2$	$^1/_{16}$	$^1/_{64}$
1 quart (qt)	2	1	$^1/_8$	$^1/_{32}$
1 peck (pk)	16	8	1	$^1/_4$
1 bushel (bu)	64	32	4	1

LIQUID 1	te	ta	oz	cup
1 teaspoon (te)	1	$^1/_3$	$^1/_6$	$^1/_{48}$
1 tablespoon (ta)	3	1	$^1/_2$	$^1/_{16}$
1 ounce (oz)	6	2	1	$^1/_8$
1 cup	48	16	8	1

LIQUID 2	pt	qt	gal	ltr
1 pint (pt)	1	$^1/_2$	$^1/_8$	.473
1 quart (qt)	2	1	$^1/_4$	.946
1 gallon (gal)	8	4	1	3.785
1 liter (ltr)	2.113	1.057	.264	1

WEIGHT	gr	dr	oz	lb
1 grain (gr)	1	.004	.003	$^1/_{7000}$
1 dram (dr)	27.34	1	$^1/_{16}$	$^1/_{256}$
1 ounce (oz)	437.5	16	1	$^1/_{16}$
1 pound (lb)	7000	256	16	1

OVEN TEMPERATURES

very low	250 – 275 degrees
low	300 – 325 degrees
moderate	350 – 375 degrees
hot	400 – 425 degrees
very hot	450 – 475 degrees
extremely hot	500 – 525 degrees
broil	550 degrees and above

0 1 2 3 4 5 6 7 8

0 1 2

Have something to demonstrate or explain? Don't say it—show it!

How to draw great visual instructions

Ever get bogged down reading a VCR manual? Assembly instructions for a toy? Directions to a food processor? It has happened to everybody. Even written in plain English, they're too verbal! For example:

> **Check the tape transport direction.**
> If necessary, press DIR. Both-sides-recording should be started from the forward (front) side. (◄ of the ◄ ► FWD/REV indicator should be lit.)

We live in a *visual* world. We pick things up, move them about, pull them, turn them, set them down. To convey directions intuitively, we need *visual* language.

We need to speak in pictures.

A secret to illustrating instructions is to trace them from snapshots you take yourself. Unlike high-quality photos, which must be carefully and expensively staged and lighted, drawing allows you to arrange and rearrange the action quickly with no regard for details. Once the snapshot is made (Polaroids are great), you are immediately free to pick out important parts, change position, exaggerate key actions, and so forth to make the message clear.

While a very simple action can be presented as a single panel, instructions are usually a multi-panel sequence of step-by-steps—do *this,* then *that,* then the *other* (above). Illustrated hands are outstanding communicators! While arrows and pointers can do the job, hands are better. Why? Because they're us. We can relate. We project ourselves into the action. And since they're generic, everyone joins in. Hand action in a sequence has another fine benefit—it appears to be moving, which is how we naturally see things.

Plan your action thoroughly. Go overboard; too many pictures are preferable to too few. Scan your snapshots. Then in your draw program, begin tracing.

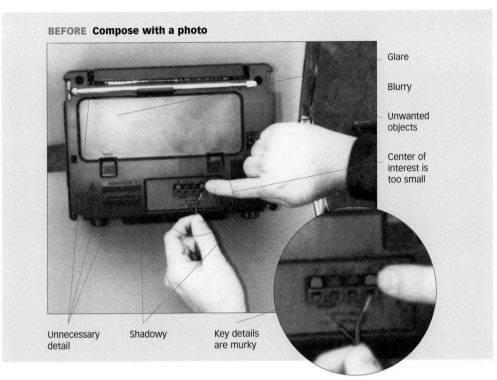

BEFORE Compose with a photo

Glare

Blurry

Unwanted objects

Center of interest is too small

Unnecessary detail

Shadowy

Key details are murky

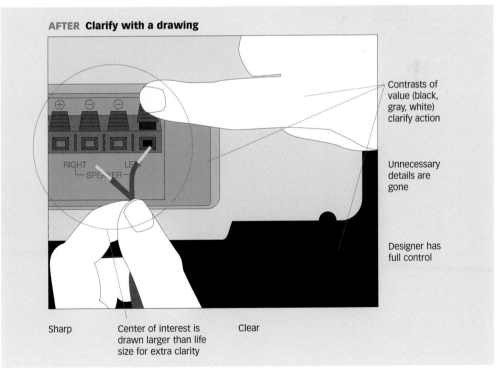

AFTER Clarify with a drawing

Contrasts of value (black, gray, white) clarify action

Unnecessary details are gone

Designer has full control

RIGHT LEFT
SPEAKER

Sharp

Center of interest is drawn larger than life size for extra clarity

Clear

1   Draw only the parts you need

Think minimum. At each step in a sequence, draw only the parts pertinent to that step—in this case a mere outline of the radio and plug-in panel. Also draw any part needed to orient the object—in other words, to clue the reader where he or she is. At right, the small rectangles in the upper corners tell the reader this is the back of the radio. Leave everything else out.

Extra parts only divide the reader's attention.

Show only what you need to. Here, the point of interest is easily located in the context of the object's outline.

2   Find the best pose

In real life you'd be likely to press the button this way—by gripping the radio so you don't push it off your desk. But this action does not translate into a clear instruction.

Hands are so expressive that every nuance conveys information, so careful work at this step is key to creating clear instructions. Be sure to *look* at the pictures you make: Although *you* know you were pushing the button, the reader won't unless you've captured the action visually. Experiment. Sometimes the most expressive action will feel awkward.

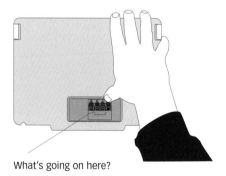

What's going on here?

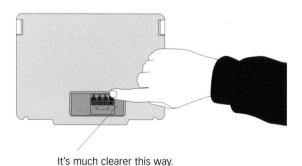

It's much clearer this way.

3 | Zoom in

Close, closer, closest. Crop to bring the action up close, but watch for two things: Leave a large enough portion of the image so as not to disorient the reader—note how the contour of the radio's bottom edge tells you where you are—and show as much of the hands as possible.

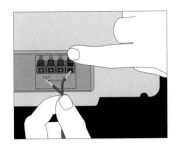

4 | Exaggerate

The inset (far right) is cropped too close—the otherwise expressive hands have been reduced to fingernails. To show detail without too-tight cropping, enlarge only a *portion* of the image; at right, only the plug-in panel is enlarged relative to the rest of the drawing.

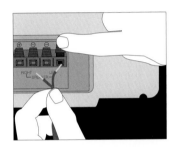

5 | Highlight

For maximum clarity, feel free to disregard your photo's natural colors or grays, and color your drawing artificially. For example, the black radio (**1**) matches the photo but the action is not sharply defined. This won't do. A lighter radio contrasts clearly with its dark plug-in panel (**2**), but its white background has no contrast with the hands. A black background (**3**) solves the problem.

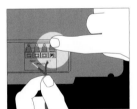

A useful way to highlight action in a dark or confined area is with a spotlight. Clone and create a lighter version of the image, then paste it inside a circle.

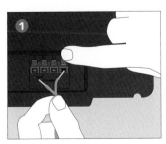 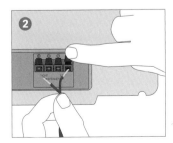 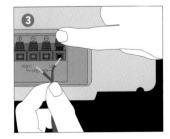

6 Reuse parts

Look for ways to use the same parts more than once. Starting from the previous image (1), the hands are easily rotated and repositioned (2) to illustrate the next step—plugging a wire into the second socket (3). Reusing parts saves drawing time, but be careful; if your old images don't express the new action with equal clarity, take another snapshot.

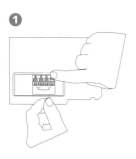

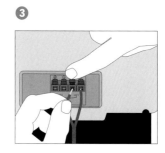

7 Modify parts

Drawing gives you the freedom to modify. The screwdriver was drawn in two pieces from separate photos, scaled to match, then spliced. It was equally easy to shorten or lengthen the shaft. Typically, you would do this to fit a space or clarify an action. You don't need to copy a photo literally.

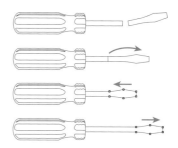

8 Explode parts

Exploded views show how parts fit together. We traced the assembled part from a photo, then added pins to the knobs and hung them in midair. For more complex objects, you may need to work from several separate photos.

An excellent way to create assembly instructions is to first show an exploded view of the parts, then follow with the steps of fitting them together.

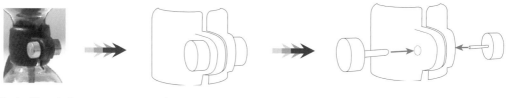

Start with a photo…   then trace…   for an exploded view.

9 Simplify parts

Think minimum. Simple drawings are best. Wherever you can simplify an object without altering the reader's perception of it, do so. At right, the threads have been reduced from three lines to two.

Good

Better

Repetitive parts, patterns, and actions can often be drawn quickly. Here, the screw shaft is drawn by duplicating a single thread.

10 Create x-ray views

Your drawings can reveal parts and actions the camera cannot see—an indispensable asset. Here, the drawing illustrates access to a recessed screw. Screwdriver and screw were combined from separate photos, which we shot on the hood of a white car.

Get all those fingers walking to your place.

How to design a Yellow Pages ad

The Yellow Pages may be one of America's most widely shopped markets, but they certainly didn't get that way because of their good looks. Cluttered, inky, and predominately artless, they are a holdover from the time when "design" meant one's choice of block or script letters, capital or small, round or square corners, one piece-o-clip-art, and a logo (if you had one), all pasted up by the phone company.

The Yellow Pages succeed, instead, on the strength of one great asset: Here, buyers are actively seeking the sellers.

A shopper comes to the Yellow Pages for help. Unguided, sometimes in a hurry, maybe under stress, he's invariably looking for a company with which he is unfamiliar. And he has no way to judge: *Is this jeweler good, or that one? Is this installer reputable? Is that service fair?*

The shopper has only our ad to go by. Does it attract? Is it clear? Do we appear helpful? Honest? Sound?

Our design can (and should convey) these attributes. If you run a good business, here's how to say so visually.

Inky-poo
A normal ad basks on clean white paper, but not in the Yellow Pages. Here it's on yellow that you can see right through (keep that in mind when planning "white" space) and surrounded by direct competitors. This is war.

Every powerful ad starts with a focal point...

The Yellow Pages are full of look-alike ads. Same typestyles, same CAPITAL LETTERS, same sizes, same borders, same colors, endlessly repeated on every Yellow Page from Maine to Hawaii. And with everything looking the same, it all runs together in a big mush.

First step is to escape this trap. Every powerful ad (Yellow Pages or not) is built around a focal point. The focal point of an ad is its dominant object, generally the biggest, boldest or brightest thing in it. It is its point of emphasis. The focal point is a visual anchor on which everything else can moor.

A focal point may be type or it may be art. The easiest way to make a focal point is to create a contrast between one object and the others. Here are six ways to do that.

Isolation
One object set apart from the others

Scale
One object much larger or smaller than the others

Color
One object a different color from the others

Group
Several objects that create one visual mass

Weight
One object much heavier or lighter than the others

Value
Grays add depth; objects come forward or recede

BEFORE

1 Isolation

A distant focal point makes two distinct zones.

It's only clip art, but this image has a lot going for it. The most powerful shape in graphic design is a circle, the most powerful force on Earth is the sun, and the most compelling sight to any reader is another human face. What we've done here is simply pushed the dominat-ing graphic away from the text. The interesting result: The words on the right now stand out, too. Set words in a column, then add your graphic and push elements to the outer edges. Bridge the gap that results by s-p-a-c-i-n-g out the name. Note (right bottom) the vertical and horizontal axes that cross roughly at eye level. Simple and slick.

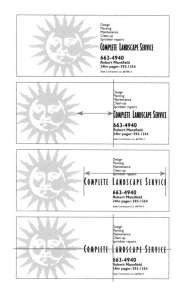

AFTER 1

Type specs
Landscape: Runic Condensed; **All other:**
Poppi-Laudatio Condensed and Bold Condensed

Super-size type anchors a simple message

An excellent solution when you have no artwork, this design uses supersize type as its focal
point. Note the organization it imposes—the
company name is now unmistakable. Its services with pertinent name and numbers follow
in a single, easy-to-read column. The reader
can take in every bit of information effortlessly.

You'll be pleased to find that at this size
many ordinary typefaces are very artistic (you'll
see this most readily in the curves). The longer
your word, the more condensed it must be, of
course.

Right, select a key word and set it quite tightly, big enough to touch top and bottom but
with room for descriptive words, then align
details in a column at the end. Watch for points
of alignment; note here it's the x-height.

We used the x-height
as a point of alignment.

Serifs meet the border
Not suitable for every typeface but great for
this one, here we've lengthened the ascenders
and descenders enough to meet the border.
This creates a visual unit that's stronger than
type left floating.

AFTER 2

3 Value

Type specs
Headline: Boulevard with Snell Roundhand initial cap; **All other:** ITC Berkeley Oldstyle Roman, Italic and Bold

Grays add layers of clarity to a wordy ad.
There's no missing the focal point here—"Beautiful Lighting" set in a beautiful script that *looks* like what it says (1). Its size dominates both the products and the company name. If yours is a physical product, strive to obtain good photos, which are nearly always more appealing than line art. We found these in a manufacturer's catalog. What makes this ad soar are its shades, or values, of gray (2), which add depth to the space and strength to its airy headline. (Note the spotlight effect.) Upper and lowercase type—always more welcoming in voice than all caps—is now centered in a beautiful serif type.

AFTER 1

1   **2**

Centered means centered on an axis, not in a space, and it normally implies *static* or stable. But here the axis is itself off center; this slight asymmetry is more dynamic than a fully centered ad.

Type specs
Headline: Copperplate 33BC; **All other:** Adobe Caslon Bold and Bold Italic

Three small photos pull like one big shot

When you want to show off your products but have more than one, pull them into a group. Here, three different and irregularly shaped lamps combine in a single focal point. The energetic, angled composition results in two natural corners for text. This technique usually works best if you first give your photos a common background, which we've done with gray squares. Overlapping the squares then ties them together. Note all the lamps are upright but the outer squares angle inward in opposite directions. This is how to keep a reader's eye moving into a space, not out of it.

AFTER 2

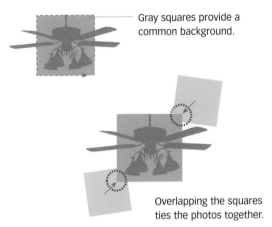

Gray squares provide a common background.

Overlapping the squares ties the photos together.

A WORD ABOUT WORDS

In the Yellow Pages, as in other kinds of advertising, design and copy work hand in hand. To be most effective, your ad must not only look good, its words must be attractive, too.

Take it for granted that a shopper on your page is interested in your product. Respect this! Give him or her useful, informative statements rather than vague claims. Avoid slogans. Instead of "We care," say, "Open 24 hours a day." Instead of "We really want your business," say, "Free 10-day trial in your home." Facts might include location—a map can be helpful—hours, selection, availability, service, experience, guarantees, and, of course, your phone number. But don't bury the shopper in detail; small amounts of well-chosen information yield the best results.

To get the biggest jump on your competition, borrow some advertising techniques from Madison Avenue. For example, include a headline. "Firm your tummy in 10 minutes a day!" will draw much more interest than "Ned's Gym and Weight Room Supply." Make sure your headline has a direct and obvious benefit for the customer.

And try writing in narrative-style sentences, too, the same as you would use in real life. "We'll have your pipes fixed in an hour" is more appealing and informative than "Pipe Repair: Fast Service."

BEFORE

The data depot

A warehouse of information is here, stocked in neat lists, too, but without variation or voice, it looks like a warehouse. Words in ALL CAPS would normally stand out, but here that won't work because EVERY WORD IS IN ALL CAPS. The green ink was an attempt to alleviate the sameness, but there's even too much of that.

In any group of objects, the one that's different will draw your eye. Note, inset right, that just by removing most of the green, the name and phone number become more prominent. This gives the eye a focal point.

---

5 Weight and color

The eye goes to the thing that's different.
Vastly simplified, the bold, black van and the light headline form a contrast of *weight* that draws attention to both. This is not only the surest way to be seen on a busy page (right), but the oversize, serif-style headline is a sophisticated challenge to the squat, newspaper style of competitors. The ad-style approach is different, too. Instead of a dull list of services, we're engaging the shopper with real questions and answers. Someone who's locked out will call this company first.

BEFORE   AFTER

Double focal point
While the van (**1**) and headline (**2**) form a contrast of weight, the red logo (**3**) creates a contrast of color. This is the best way to use the primitive color in the Yellow Pages. Simply apply it to your most important item. The more often you use it, the more diluted its effect.

AFTER 1

Three small ads instead of one big one

In advertising, repetition is everything. The Yellow Pages sometimes recommend running your ad more than once. A smart and economical way to do this is to divide a big ad into several small ones, each promoting one aspect of the business. Here, identical format and typography create an unmistakable series, each ad reinforcing the other. The single bold graphic and red logo pull so hard that on a page the new ad rivals the original "before" version (below), even though it's only one-third its size. This series could be run on successive pages, or scattered around one page, or even stacked or clustered on one page. Note in each case the graphic object breaks out of the ad's hairline border.

Type specs
Headline: ITC Century Light Condensed;
Description type: ITC Century Bold Condensed;
Logo: Industria Solid and ITC Kabel Bold;
Address: Helvetica Neue 65 Medium;
Phone number: Helvetica Neue 95 Black

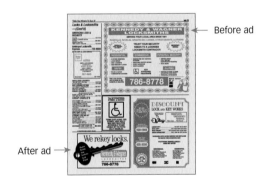

← Before ad

After ad →

AFTER 2

Charts, Reports, Calendars, & Maps

The perfect *point map* will guide the reader anywhere without a word of text.

Bring the world to your door

The most valuable business map is the *point map*—that is, the map that guides the reader to the specific destination—a mall, your office, the annual convention site. A point map differs from a topographic map, which is an accurate depiction of an area's geography and includes political boundaries, rivers, and so forth.

A topographic map shows everything. On a point map, all that matters is the destination. A designer, therefore, is not restricted to geography. He or she can move mountains, reroute interstates, even erase whole cities for the sake of clear communication. This can be a great deal of fun because, once the transportation problem has been solved, the designer has vast freedom with the map's appearance. Here's how to produce a greatly simplified map to an office in Sacramento.

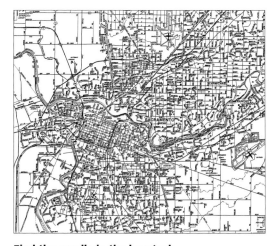

Find the needle in the haystack
Welcome to the Sacramento metropolitan area! Over one hundred thousand homes, the state capitol (and attendant sprawl), a professional sports complex, two Air Force bases, and a railroad museum are among the objects hidden in the scan above. The office we are seeking is here, too, tiny as a pinpoint.

When designing a point map, take plenty of time to think the problem through—the more you do, the less the reader must do. This is especially important if you are, say, a retailer trying to attract shoppers to your store. Think first: *What is the most direct route there?*

1 Cut through the clutter

Our destination is the red dot downtown. We started by pitching everything but the freeways—rivers, paths, points of interest, landmarks, everything. This is a common first step. Everyone has access to a freeway, and in this case, the freeways all lead downtown.

   This initial editing is critical and can be a bear. Look again at the original map: It is easy (and normal) to be distracted by the sheer volume of the graphical information in front of you. It may help to close your eyes and imagine giving oral instructions to a lost motorist: "Straight three blocks, right at the light, third door on the left." Let the rest of the world vanish.

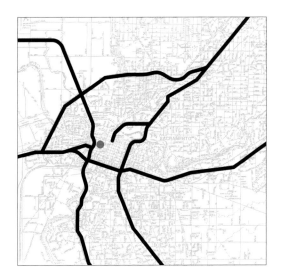

2 Define the target

Freeways cover the big distances in a few strokes; the last few miles require detail. In this case, we added a downtown grid. It does not need to be street-for-street accurate and will change as the map evolves. (Note that the downtown streets are white on a neutral background. If you have the luxury of high-resolution output, make *all* movement corridors lighter than the background and all impenetrable objects, such as buildings, darker than the background. The eye will thereby separate them instantly.) The map has now been stripped to the three key pieces: the long distances, the short distances, and the target.

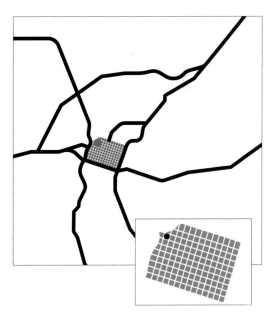

3 | Simplify

Next, straight lines replace wiggly ones. This is done to simplify the information, to clue the user that this is a schematic, and help him visualize in forms that he can better remember than the twists and turns of geographic reality. For ease of drawing, the map has been rotated level and centered on our target. Doing so made it evident that downtown is boxlike, a feature we can build upon. Watch for similar characteristics to emerge on other maps.

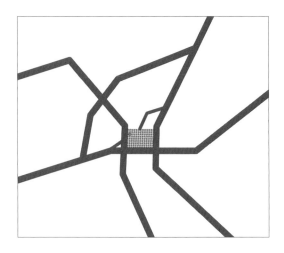

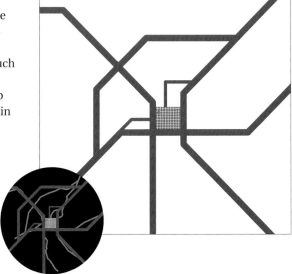

Find the angle

This rotation step is temporary (it's easier to draw things upright) so we need to know the angle to unrotate it later. Here's how: Hold the Shift key while you draw a horizontal line across your map. Rotate the line by eye until it aligns with an angled map edge. Make a note of the angle as shown in your program's palette.

4 | 45-degree angle clarify

Horizontal, vertical and 45-degree strokes (merely hold the Shift key as you click) reduce the map to its essence: a pure schematic diagram that will put the user at ease. (It's cool looking, too—because it's so orderly.) With such severe constraints, it is surprisingly easy to mimic reality. The overlay compares this map to the original. Doubling the width of the main freeways distinguishes them from the small entrance highways, but they're so bold they would overpower everything if not shaded 75 percent black.

5 It's neat, but how to show detail?

It is at this point a map is likeliest to fail. The main map covers the same 250 square miles as the original, which means the destination is still too small to be seen. The solution? Enlarging a section into a second map (inset) is common but works only if the section is an isolated one (showing, say, a restaurant district within a larger map). In this case, it is not: The downtown must link with its freeways at nine points, and the details of those links are crucial. Designing such detail in two sizes and expecting the reader to compare them is abysmal. It may look good, but it's infuriating to decipher.

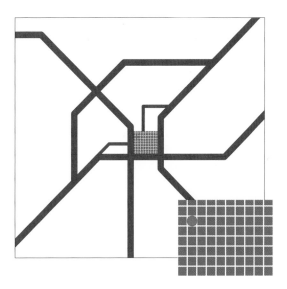

6 Use the principle of *variable scale*

This technique sounds a bit complicated, but it is amazing. So far, the map has been pictured at a scale of about 6:1; that is, one inch equals six miles. Here, we enlarged *only the downtown* 300 percent (an arbitrary amount that looked right). One inch now equals only two downtown miles—but still six miles everywhere else. To do so required squeezing the immediate freeways outward (the map has been redrawn again), yet the outermost points have barely moved. The solution is fabulous: The map still covers 250 square miles, yet the target is now in view and navigable.

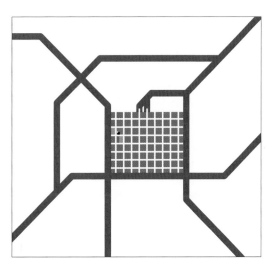

Once variable scale had been applied, the sharp-angled freeways took on the appearance of ordinary streets. Since freeways arc and sweep rather than jut and jab, rounded bends restored a sense of distance and expanse—the way we perceive them from our cars. the rounded intersections are you-can-turn-this-way clues that leave a driver no doubt how the freeways link.

Downtown has many more streets than the grid shows, but we don't care; our only interest is in the important streets *which lead to the office* (not to be mistaken for the biggest streets). All others get the ax. Critical freeway exits are made by splicing on quarter-circles (note the two radii).

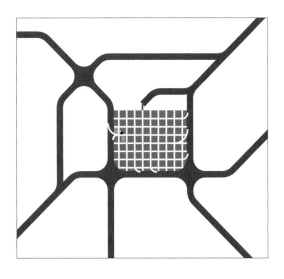

An easy way to add rounded intersections:

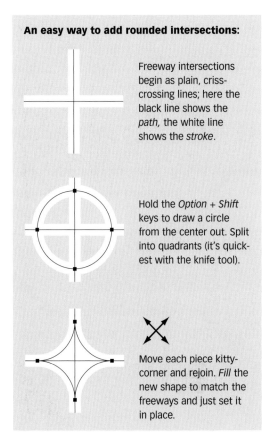

Freeway intersections begin as plain, criss-crossing lines; here the black line shows the *path,* the white line shows the *stroke.*

Hold the *Option + Shift* keys to draw a circle from the center out. Split into quadrants (it's quickest with the knife tool).

Move each piece kitty-corner and rejoin. *Fill* the new shape to match the freeways and just set it in place.

How to round off the 45-degree bends:

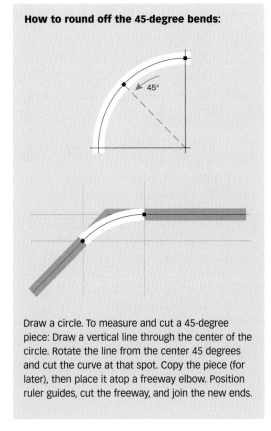

Draw a circle. To measure and cut a 45-degree piece: Draw a vertical line through the center of the circle. Rotate the line from the center 45 degrees and cut the curve at that spot. Copy the piece (for later), then place it atop a freeway elbow. Position ruler guides, cut the freeway, and join the new ends.

We're not done yet. All roads must converge on the destination. Here, the only streets still on the map are connected to the desired office or to a freeway exit—and the untraveled parts colored to recede. Note how evenly the streets are spaced. That's variable scale again: The distance, for example, from 3rd to 5th Streets, then 5th to 10th Streets, is the same.

Standard U.S. highway signs are clear and universally recognized. Why didn't we use them? Because the map is so stylized they would have looked out of place, nerd-like, in a   sea of cool. Allowing form to overrule function like this is risky.

The only way to pull it off is to restore the function. In this case, using "CA 00" works well for state highways, as does "US 00" for federal highways, and "I 00" for interstates. These abbreviations make an implicit connection between the labels and the funny-shaped signs that are actually on the roads.

The yellow dots, however, are a one-of-a-kind solution. If your street is the Langendorf Plaza Parkway, you'll have to think of something else.

This map uses color, but these techniques would work well in black and white, too—especially at high resolution. Below, the irregular green background is a cosmetic addition, a stylized version of the city limits.

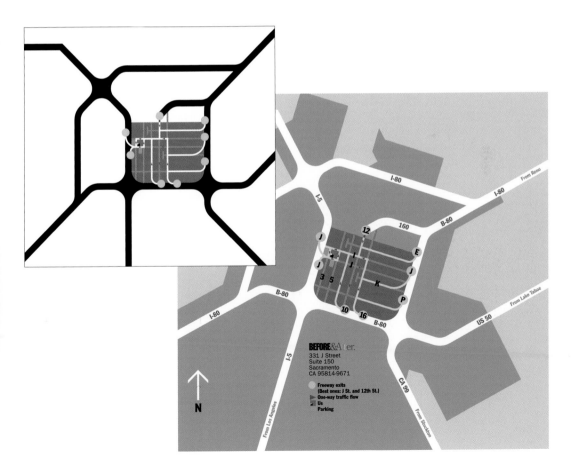

Perfect for your desk, monitor, or wall.

A single line of months and days

What an unexpected calendar this is! It's a month presented in a single line of numbers differentiated only by type weight and color—weekdays in one, weekends in the other. It labels no days of the week, and yet it's obvious which day is which and where the holidays are. What could be simpler or sleeker? Its minimalist line makes it a beautiful desk calendar. You can tape it to your monitor, or put it on your wall. The challenge of creating this cool calendar, however, is to maintain its simplicity: It would be easy to complicate it unnecessarily. The key choices you have are typestyle, type weight, color, value, and iconography. Have a look.

Typestyle Helvetica 11/5 pt   **Type weights** Black and light   **Icon**   **Colors** Black, white, and red

February 04   **1** 2 3 4 5 6 **7 8** 9 10 11 12 13 **14 15** 16 17 18 19 20 **21 22** 23 24 25 26 27 **28 29**

Values Black and white on middle value

The keys to simplicity

Color value

You'll get the richest results using values of light, dark, and neutral. This will allow contrast between all of the items on the calendar—background, weekdays, weekends, and special days. Your office printer will handle some colors and values better than others. Experiment.

1 Helvetica Light and Black have real weight contrast, and colored black and white, they have value contrast, too. Bold white type is most visible, so weekends stand out. A simple dot distinguishes a special day.

2 This is set simply in Utopia, a standard text typeface. A lighter-than-usual background hides the weekends, making weekdays most prominent. The rocket is homemade.

3 Classic Garamond type in one weight separates days by color value only. This is handsome, but harder to "read." This easy design uses no icons; month and special days are on a reversed field.

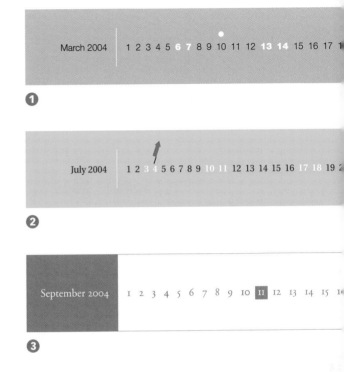

Simple type

Keep your typeface simple. Classics are always good. Contrasting bold and light weights are preferable but not necessary. Avoid detailed faces, which are lost at small sizes.

Simple icons

Special days can be marked with an icon; dingbat and picture fonts are a good source. You can also make your own—it's fun.

Yes No

Complex Better Best

Here's a new twist: It's easy to make in the office. Just set up the template as shown, print on heavy stock, cut and fold. A new image every month, plus a message on the back, makes the calendar an excellent giveaway, keepsake, or reminder. It's suitable for family mementos, vacation photos, all kinds of things. It's very clean, with no ruled lines that normally clutter a calendar: Any image looks great. Note here that the white calendar portion is truly black-on-white minimal. Weekends stand apart in type weight only.

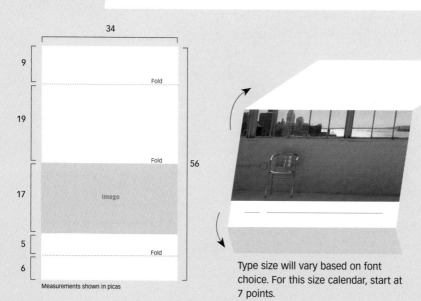

Measurements shown in picas

Type size will vary based on font choice. For this size calendar, start at 7 points.

Overlap the flaps slightly— enough to make the back straight (more or less)— and secure with tape.

How to improve the type you set

Ever wonder why there are so many different typefaces? It's because we've got so many different things to say! Natural conversation is full of pauses, shifts in emphasis, and points of interest. Your goal in typesetting is to impart these characteristics visually.

Highlights

ENTRY: Window beside door keeps entry bright. Oak parquet floor and finished wood stairway make entry very appealing.
LIVING ROOM: Newer beige-color carpeting and draperies, and has a nice, open feeling.
KITCHEN: New almond-color stove, refrigerator and fan hood, lots of oak cabinets, ample counter space.

Highlights

ENTRY: Window beside door keeps entry bright. Oak parquet floor and finished wood stairway make entry very appealing.

LIVING ROOM: Newer beige color carpeting and draperies, and has a nice, open feeling.

KITCHEN: New almond-color stove, refrigerator and fan hood, lots of oak cabinets, ample counter space.

BEFORE
Clipped from a real estate flier, this hasty bit of typesetting contradicts its own words. The idea was excellent: to describe a house for sale in a way that would attract the shopper who had not yet seen it. But while the words speak of bright, pleasant lighting, an open feeling, and ample space, they appear dank, crowded, unwelcoming. This is because type has been poured in with no attention to *voice*.

AFTER
Now the words look like what they say: bright, open, airy, pretty—and the reader is very likely to transfer these now-visible qualities to the house in his mind's eye. What has made the difference? A lot has changed.

Unless you've got snake oil to sell, text should speak in a calm, natural voice. Select the text face first; try starting with a light serif. Changes in subject require contrast; for this, a heavy sans serif always works. Text that's justified (before) is like a prepared speech; a ragged right margin (after) is conversational and, as a rule, more inviting.

Lower x-height
10-point Caslon (after) is better than 10-point Palatino (before) because of its lower x-height; crowded Palatino seems harried. Alternative: add more leading.

LIVING ROOM: New carpeting and drap a nice, open feelin

Use hanging indents
Dictionary-style heads embellish and are extremely easy to read. Think of them as hand gestures.

ROOM: Newer

Reduce cap size
Bold heads clearly change the subject. Bold capitals impart a firm, fatherly tone, but at full size they SHOUT; you don't want that. Reduce them 1 to 2 points and tint gray—here, 70%.

12-pt.	entry br
12-pt.	and finis
12-pt.	entry ve
16-pt.	**LIVING RC**
12-pt.	carpetin

Add extra space between paragraphs
This creates a tiny pause, like taking a breath before moving on. The more space, the longer the pause; for a stop, skip a line.

Bring customers to your door with just a few words. | By Chuck Green

Create a word map

Expecting guests? Customers? Do they know
where to find you? If not, here's a novel idea:
Fax or e-mail them a sheet of written directions. This "word map" has space for multiple
starting points, estimated travel time, and other
tips, but its real asset is the way it guides the
reader step by step, just like you would do in
person, no matter what the route.

   Travel the routes yourself to make the most
accurate map possible; you might also draft a
friend to do the same, just to make sure. When
the map is done, you'll have more time to con-
duct business, spend less time giving directions
over the phone, and your guests won't waste
time driving in circles.

Word map layout
1 Title: Franklin Gothic Bold Condensed, 16-pt., align
left; **Subtitle:** Franklin Gothic Book Condensed,
13-pt., align left; **2 Headline:** Franklin Gothic Bold
Condensed, 13-pt., align left; **3 Text:** Franklin Gothic
Book Condensed, 13/12-pt., align left.

Traveling to Example Corporation
987 Sampler Way, Building 6, Sampler Valley, North Carolina

Need more info?
987-555-3210

Traveling south on Interstate 12 . . .

Recommendations: Estimated travel time: 10 minutes from exit 345. Far left lane of Interstate 12 is restricted to High Occupancy Vehicles (HOV) with three or more occupants between 6:30 am and 9:00 am, Monday through Friday. Add a minimum of 30 minutes to your travel time between these hours.

Turn	At	Onto	For	Instructions
exit 345, north		Example Drive, north	1.5 miles	stay in left lane
left	end of Example Drive	Sampler Blvd.	.25 mile	
left	Sampler Store (on right)	Example Street	.5 mile	
bear right	railroad tracks	Highway 67	4 miles	
right	just beyond church (on right)	Sampler Way	100 yards	2nd building on right. Spaces 1–15
987 Sampler Way Building 6		Elevator	1	2th floor

From the Sampler Valley International Airport . . .

Recommendations: Estimated travel time: 40 minutes from airport entrance. Our office and the airport are both on the same side of town, so you will avoid the heaviest traffic. However, you should add 10 minutes to your travel time between 4 pm and 6 pm, Monday through Friday.

Turn	At	Onto	For	Instructions
		Example Blvd., north	.5 mile	stay in right lane
right	interstate on-ramp	Interstate 56 east	5 miles	
exit 345, north		Interstate 78, north	12.5 miles	
exit 23, west		Highway 67	4 miles	(continued...)

A good chart communicates quickly. Here's how to make one.

What's at the heart of a chart?

Data of any kind is easier to understand once we *see* it. The following charts picture the growth of junk bonds over a specific period of time. The six variations are practically identical: same bars, same data, same size—even the proportions are the same. Each was created using only line and box tools, and yet the results are decidedly different.

In narrative form, the data looks like this: *Bonds outstanding, in billions: 2001, $82;* *2002, $126; 2003, $159; 2004, $180.* The numbers are easy enough to understand. You'd chart this data for only one reason: to aid comprehension *of a trend.* Once the designer understands this, he or she can create a simple chart that's easier to read and understand than the text. But the sheer number of graphic tools in front of you conspire to draw your eye from the task at hand. It's important to stay focused.

1 Menu shock

This chart will stop the most avid reader. Rather than accelerate comprehension—in this case, of a simple trend—it seriously interferes. For example, the dollar scale forces the reader to *stop, follow a line to the bottom,* and *estimate* an amount. And why make the reader compare legend patterns *for no reason but to learn the year each bar represents?* The outlined headline muddies rather than clarifies, and the bold patterns are as brash as polka dots and plaid.

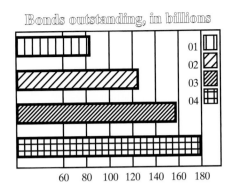

Bonds outstanding, in billions

2 Four steps in the right direction

At least you don't need sunglasses to view this version. Every box and outline was superfluous; the bars are sufficient to define themselves, and the smooth, gray tones allow the reader to absorb the *data,* not the graphics. Years placed adjacent to their bars (rather than the typical legend) speed comprehension a lot. Four vertical lines drop to their exact dollar amounts and communicate directly. Note that each bar is atop the vertical lines that do not pertain to it, adding clarity.

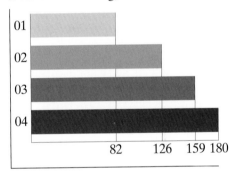

Bonds outstanding, in billions

3 Two problems solved

This chart is less attractive than the previous one, but it communicates as fast because the dollar amounts are right in the bars. The reader now has a straight reading path from year to dollar while the length of the bars tells the story visually—that is, that the dollar amounts rose steadily. Note there is no need to color the bars differently since each conveys the same *kind* of information. Copiers don't reproduce tints well; simple lines like these work better in such cases.

Bonds outstanding, in billions

2001	$82
2002	$126
2003	$159
2004	$180

4 This chart will pull the eye

Reversing the image creates a bold, clean graphic that will draw the eye amidst any amount of clutter. It is flawed because the graphic now overpowers the font, which suddenly looks meek (it is unchanged); even so, it conveys its information rapidly. Not only is it better, but it is easier to make than the chart shown first. The bar lengths do not have to be precise since they include their own data: Just get reasonably close.

BONDS OUTSTANDING, IN BILLIONS	
2001	$82
2002	$126
2003	$159
2004	$180

5 Contrasts in type and shade clarify

The best-looking chart on the page is also the best chart. *Every element aids comprehension.* Set in two fonts, Helvetica Black and Light, variations in size, weight, and color make each kind of data similar (which provides visual continuity) yet unique (which provides clarity). The dollar amounts are huge and bold, yet in white on gray, they recede proportionately. Comprehension is instantaneous. This is a perfect chart.

6 An excellent chart shifts the emphasis

Recoloring the previous chart throws the balance to the data bars and makes the banner recede. Note the vertical gray background stripes; these *suggest* data—all that's needed here. On another chart they could be real number lines. Note also how the banner is pristine (a function of its uppercase letters) while the Helvetica Black and Light fonts contrast and elegantly rank its information by importance.

Design a "photo" graph

Add professional-caliber appeal to your next chart the easy way—by laying it atop a photograph. Effective in both black and white and in color, this treatment is much more expressive than plain data, and it's as easy as it looks. Look for a photo with a detail-free area, and keep your chartwork simpler than usual—plain bars, lines and dots are best.

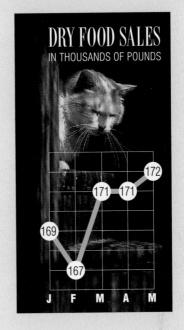

To use a backdrop photo...
Many photographs are suitable for charts. To avoid distracting busyness, the area behind your chart should have little or no detail, and the chart itself should be fairly plain.

As a rule, make your chart as large as possible in the space available.

Keys to success: organization and a smart sense of style.

How to design a business report

No document is better suited to desktop publishing than the common business report. Artistically less demanding than a newsletter, a business report is a low-key compilation of data on a single subject, directed to an extremely limited audience of interested readers.

In a business report, *information is everything.* And information will profit from an organized, visually refined presentation. The report that looks professional—clear, accessible and disciplined—is persuasive.

The model shown here is intended for output on one-sided, laser-printed sheets. Use or discard pages as necessary—for example, you may not need a table of contents. This sample was designed to be a versatile foundation that will see you through many reports and board meetings.

Read this entire article before you begin your design. It helps to understand at each phase what to expect in the next.

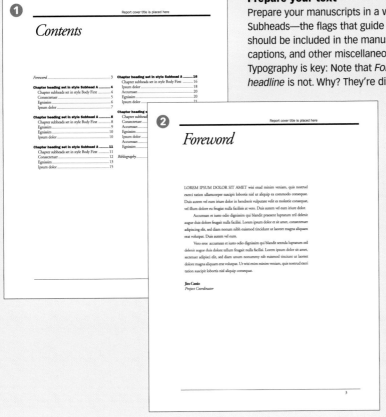

Prepare your text

Prepare your manuscripts in a word processing program. Subheads—the flags that guide readers through the data—should be included in the manuscripts as they occur: Headlines, captions, and other miscellaneous text will be added later. Typography is key: Note that *Foreword* is italicized; *Chapter headline* is not. Why? They're different kinds of information.

1 Contents are useful for a long or detailed subject; this example is divided by chapter and subheads. Leader dots are found in tab settings. Note the fonts.

2 Long lines demand deeper leading. Here, the standard 13 points have been increased to 18. If *Contents* and *Foreword* are short, try combining them on a single page.

---

1 Set up the page

Margins, columns and ruler guides form a grid upon which the report is built. *This is a sophisticated grid of right-hand-only pages.* Go through the steps, and as you become familiar with its structure, the function of each guide will become clear.

Document setup
Page: Letter size, portrait orientation; single-sided; **Baseline grid:** 13-pt.; **Margins:** Left, 7p0; Right, 7p0; Top 8p8; Bottom, 6p5; **Column guides:** 2 columns, 1p0 between; **Guides:** Horizontal ruler guides at 4p0, 16p0, 57p0; Vertical ruler guides at 7p0, 8p0, 27p0, 35p6, 36p6, 47p0; **End lines:** 4-pt. line at 4p0, hairline at 57p0.

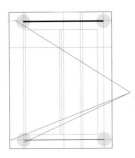

After rules are drawn, horizontal guides 4p0, 57p0, vertical guide 7p0 may be discarded.

Select two type families; a light serif face for text and headlines, and a very bold sans serif face for contrasting subheads and the cover. Create your paragraph styles as shown on the next page.

TIP

If you don't have our fonts: Times and Palatino are useful substitutes for Garamond but should be set one point size smaller (same leading). Use Futura extra bold or Helvetica Black for Franklin Gothic. The report can also be set entirely in Bookman—substitute bold for Franklin Gothic—but set text two points smaller.

ADOBE GARAMOND

FRANKLIN GOTHIC HEAVY

Standard text page is the most common in the report—subheads and sub-subheads are critical visual breaks. Write them carefully. Graphics are placed to the right and down.

A bibliography is a type of index. Set the author's name in bold, book (or paper) title in italics. Note that each report *title* page begins at the same ruler level. Consistency matters.

Chapter headline ⑤
is placed here

④ **Subhead A appears to hang over column**

① Lorem ipsum dolor sit amet, consectetur adipscing elit, diam nonnumy eiusmod tempor incidunt ut labore et dolore magna aliquam erat volupat. Ut enim ad minimim veniami quis en nostrud exercitation ullamcorper suscipit laboris nisl ut aliquip ex ea commodo consequat.

Duis autem vel eum ipsum irure dolor in reprehenderit in voluptate velital esse molestaie son consequat, vel illum dolore eu fugiat nulla-pariatur. At vero eos et accusam etam justo odio dignissim qui blandit praesent lupatum delenit aigue duos dolor et molestais conpur exceptur sint occaecat cupidat non provident, simil tempor sunt in culpa qui officia de serunt mollit anim id est laborum et dolor fugai.

Et harumd dereud facilis estum expedit distinct nam liber ament tempor. Cum soluta nobis eligend op tio comque nihil quod a impedit anim id quod max im placeat facer possim omnis es voluptas as sumen da est, omnis dolor repellend. Temporem eutemat quinsud et aur office debit aut tum rerum necessit atib saepe eveniet ut er repudiand sint et molestia nonum este recusand. Itaque earud rerum hic tentury sapiente delectus au aut prefer endis dolorib asperiore repellat.

③ *This is an example of Subhead B*

Hanc ego cum tene sentniam, quid est cur verear ne ad eam non possing accommodare nost ros quos tu paulo ante cum memorite it tum etia ergat. Et harumd dereud facilis dolor vontae.

Nos amice et nebevol, olestias access potest fier ad augendas cum conscient to et factor tum toen legum odioque civiuda. Et tamen in busdad ne que pecun modut est neque nonor imper ned libiding gen epular religuard on cupiditat, quas nullam praid im umdna etano en magist and et dodecend ense vide antur, invitat igtur ratio.

Pariatur ad iustitiami aequitated fidem. Neque hominy infant aut inuiste fact est cond que neg facile efficerd possit duo conteud notiner si effecerit, ops vel forunag veling en libaralitat mag is em conveniunt, dabut tutungbene volent sib conciliant et, al is adtissim est ad quiet. ②

Subhead A appears to hang over column
Subhead B may appear beneath Subhead A

Endium caritat praesert cum omning null sillicaus peaccand quaerer en imigent cupidat a natura proficis facile explent sinela julla inura autend unanc sunt isti nulla en consequat lorem kuntilla pullat. Uta enim ad minimim veniami quis nostrud exercitation ullamcorper suscipit lab oris nisl aliquip ex com-modo consequat.

Lorem aute vellum irure dolor in reprehend erit voluptate velt es son consequat vel illum et do lore fugiat nulla pariatur. At averot os et justo odio dignissim blandit praese nait luptatum deletal en-duo dolor et exceptur occ aecat cupidat nom provi dent, simil tempor in cul qui officia deserunt mol-lit anim id est labor um et doloresae fugai. Et har umd dereud facilis estal

This caption is set flush left in 10.5 point Adobe Garamond, on 13 points of leading. ⑦

er expedit distinct. namun liber a tempor soluta nobis eligend optio comque nihil quod a impedit anim id quod maxim placeat facer possim omnis es voluptas assumenda est, omnis dolor repellend. Temporem eutem quinsud et aur office debit aut tum rerum necessit atib saepe eveniet ut er

Style	Type					Paragraph		
Name	**Based on**	**Next**	**Font**	**Size**	**Leading**	**Left**	**First**	**Align**
1 Body	No style	Same style	Garamond	11	13	1p0	2p0	Justify
2 Body First	Body	Body	Garamond	11	13	1p0	0p0	Justify
3 Subhead B	No style	Body	Garamond Bold Italic	11	13	1p0	1p0	Left
4 Subhead A	No style	Body	Franklin Gothic Heavy	9.5	13	0p0	0p0	Left
5 Headline	No style	Same style	Garamond	44	44	0p0	0p0	Left
6 Title	No Style	Same style	Franklin Gothic Book	9.5	13	0p0	0p0	Left
7 Caption	Body	Same style	Garamond Italic	10.5	13	0p0	0p0	Left
8 Folio	No style	Same style	Garamond	11	13	0p0	0p0	Left

The report pages can be built in any order but typically begin with the heart of the report—that is, the main headline and text pages. Contents, bibliography, and the cover can come later. As you work, take special care with the typographic details.

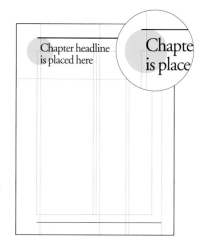

Set the first line *baseline* on the top margin guide as shown, aligned left with the 8p0 vertical ruler guide.

Set a headline

Set the headlines in the report's body typestyle—in this case, Adobe Garamond—one or two lines deep.

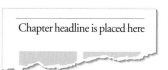

Though the headline fits on one line...

it will read better if it's set in two.

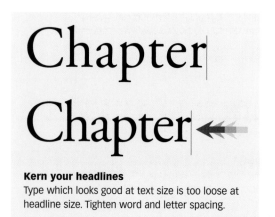

Kern your headlines
Type which looks good at text size is too loose at headline size. Tighten word and letter spacing.

Flow the text, then apply styles

This blueprint provides four manuscript *styles*: Body, Body First, Subhead A, and Subhead B. If your report will include subheads, set them beforehand as part of your manuscript so they'll flow with it. Then on the page, flow text in the usual fashion and apply styles afterward.

On pages with headlines (including contents, foreword, and bibliography), flow text from the left margin at ruler mark 16p0.

Chapter headline
is placed here

Lorem ipsum dolor sit amet, consectetur adipiscing elit, diam nonnumy eiusmod tempor incid
ut labore et dolore magna aliquam erat volupat.
Ut enim minimim veniami quis en nostrud exe
citation ullamcorper laboris aliquip ex consequat.
  Duis autem vel eum ipsum irure dolor in
voluptate velital esse son consequat, vel illum do
lore eu fugiat nulla pariatur. At vero eos et etam
justo odio dignissim qui blandit praesent lupatum
delenit aigue duos dolor et molestais conpur excep
tur sint occaecat cupidat non provident, simil
tempor sunt in culpa qui officia de serunt mollit
anim id est laborum et dolor fugai.
  Et harumd dereud facilis estum expedit distinct nam liber ament tempor. Soluta nobis eligend optio comque nihil a impedit anim id quod
max im placeat facer possim omnis es voluptas as
est, omnis dolor repellend. Temporem euteram
quinsud et aur office debit aut tum rerum necessit
atib saepe eveniet ut er repudiand sint et molestia
nonum este recusand. Itaque earud rerum tentury
sapiente delectus prefer endis dolorib asperiore.

Align text block to left margin but note text indents 1 pica.

Lorem ipsum dolor sit amet
cing elit, diam nonnumy et
Ut labore et dolore magnan
citation ullamcorper laborin
  Duis autem vel eum i:
voluptate velital esse son co
lore eu fugiat nulla pariatur
justo odio dignissim qui bla

Subhead A appears to hang
  Lorem ipsum dolor si
cing elit, diam nonnumy et
Ut labore et dolore magnan
citation ullamcorper laborin

Subhead B aligns with the
  Duis autem vel eum i:
voluptate velital esse son co
lore eu fugiat nulla pariatur
justo odio dignissim qui bla

Body first
If a first paragraph has no subhead, apply the style *Body First*, which has no first-line indent. (Don't be surprised when you see the 1-pica left margin indent, a characteristic of the style.)

Body
The standard manuscript style; apply to all following paragraphs. Note the 1-pica left margin indent and the 2-pica first-line indent.

Subhead A
The major subhead. Style abuts left margin (this is referred to as a *hanging indent*). Subhead A should be preceded by a blank line and is followed by the style *Body*.

Subhead B
The minor subhead aligns with the text. It is also preceded by a blank line and followed by the style *Body*.

Add the graphics

Graphics include photographs, illustrations, figures, tables, and charts. While a graphic conveys editorial information in pictures, it also forms a visual "mass" or weight with which our blueprint is concerned. It is useful to note that the caption that accompanies a graphic is the most important text on the page—it will be read first and most avidly (pack it with information)—and should be treated as part of the graphic.

On pages with headlines, place graphics to the outside and down; this offsets the weight of the headline.

About that funny margin
This blueprint has a narrow right margin into which graphics may extend. It serves as a visual counterweight—throwing mass to the outside—and relieves the gray monotony of the report's text margins.

Alignment is very important
The elegance of a page layout is likeliest to be spoiled by misaligned graphics and captions. What you want is a margin of one pica at the top and sides of your graphics, and two line spaces under the caption.

Place the graphic against the vertical ruler guide as shown and carefully align top and bottom with the *baseline* of the neighboring text (it may need to be cropped slightly), then align the caption.

This caption is set flush left in 10.5 point Adobe Garamond, on 13 points of leading.

Fill the column

The page's grid is invisible, but its structure is evident from the text that fills and defines its columns. Maintain that presence with your graphics and captions.

Layout suggestions
Note in each case how the graphics remain at or near the bottom; some make use of the narrow margin; others do not.

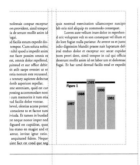

Don't float the graphic as if you were framing a picture. The result will seem weak and indecisive.

Instead, preserve the structure of the page by widening the graphic to fill its column…

or widening a substantial portion of the graphic. Here, the black box defines the space.

On pages without headlines, flow text from the top margin.

Copy short? End page evenly.
If your text falls short of filling a page, break the columns evenly for a more finished look.

The cover

A report cover should appear businesslike, direct, and answer at least two questions: What is this report? Who is it from? With no need to entertain or advertise, use type as graphics to convey not only the content but the visual interest, too. Suggestions:

Keep it simple
Visual continuity is important. To maintain it, use the two type families you used inside, then heighten their contrasts. How? By manipulating size and value (black/gray). Note, for example, how the bold title contrasts with the airy, gray serif name and date.

Type is the graphic
(Left) The huge date makes a handsome statement, its weight offset by the smaller but blacker title. Not just any typeface will do: At this size, look for graceful curves. At the bottom, three categories of information form a neat base on a three-column grid.

(Right) Note the interaction of weight (light/heavy) and value (black/gray). While not as dramatic, centered type is perfectly acceptable—and *lots* easier to do well.

Hazardous area

Very narrow columns of justified type—the kind illustrated here—need your keen eye. They tend to leave unsightly "rivers" of space between the words.

My preferred solution is to edit. One can also adjust word- and letter-spacing to allow the spaces to s-t-r-e-t-c-h and compress more than usual.

> Lorem ipsum dolor sit amet, consectetur cing elit, diam nonnumy eiusmod tempor. Ut labore dolore magna aliquam erat citation ullamcorper laborisali volupat. Duis autem vel eum irure dolor sit in voluptate velital son

Index

The look and function of everything we see benefits from design. Subscribe to Before & After, the how-to magazine for visual communicators!

If you like what you found in this book, you'll love Before & After magazine. Each issue is packed with powerful solutions to improve the visual impact of your communication materials. There is no other design resource like Before & After magazine. Before & After magazine will show you, step-by-step, how to apply design principles and make the best design decisions for your project. With Before & After magazine, you will:

• Learn the techniques of better visual communication
• Understand why things look the way they do
• Find inspiration and fresh ideas
• Discover tips for creating professional visual techniques

Subscribe online at www.bamagazine.com

Before&After
How to design cool stuff

www.bamagazine.com